SPIRIT GIFTING

Second Edition

Spirit Gifting

The Concept of Spiritual Exchange

Second Edition

Elmer Ghostkeeper, M.A.

Writing On Stone Press
PO Box 259, Raymond, AB T0K 2S0
(403) 752-4800
www.writingonstone.ca

Published by:
Writing on Stone Press Inc.
P.O. Box 259
Raymond, Alberta, Canada T0K 2S0
(403) 752-4800
Fax: (403) 752-4815
Email: info@writingonstone.ca
Web: http://www.writingonstone.ca

LIBRARY AND ARCHIVES CANADA
CATALOGUING IN PUBLICATION

Ghostkeeper, Elmer, 1947-
Spirit gifting : the concept of spiritual exchange /
Elmer Ghostkeeper. -- 2nd ed.

Includes bibliographical references and index.
ISBN 0-9781309-3-6 (pbk.)

1. Métis--Philosophy.
2. Métis--Employment--Alberta--Paddle Prairie.
3. Métis--Alberta--Paddle Prairie--Social conditions.
4. Paddle Prairie (Alta.)--History.
I. Title.

FC109.G48 2007   305.897   C2007-900769-4

DEDICATION

"Spirit Gifting" is dedicated to my parents, my father Adolphus Ghostkeeper (1893 – 1989) and my mother Elsie Ghostkeeper (1911 – 1995), and to Kim, my twin sons Jonathon and Joel, and my daughter Winter. Without their spirituality and support, I would not have had the courage and determination to complete this manuscript.

TABLE OF CONTENTS

TABLE OF FIGURES

PREFACE

THE concept of spiritual exchange known as "Spirit Gifting" (*Mekiachahkwewin*) has great value to the Metis of Paddle Prairie, Alberta. Between 1960 and 1976, a major shift in the pattern of livelihoods occurred in the community. The events of 1960 describe a livelihood that involved a sacred relationship: living *with* the land; those of 1976 involve a secular relationship: living *off* the land.

Changes in subsistence patterns caused some of the Metis of Paddle Prairie, including me, to repress their sacred worldview and the way they related through spiritual exchange with the land. In my own case, this resulted in dissatisfaction so intense that it stimulated me to attempt to revitalize my repressed worldview.

In an anthropological perspective, what happened to me parallels for individuals the group revitalization model proposed by Anthony Wallace.

ACKNOWLEDGEMENTS

I wish to acknowledge the members of my thesis committee: Dr. Michael Asch, Department of Anthropology, University of Alberta; Dr. John Foster, Department of History, University of Alberta; Michael Robinson, Arctic Institute of North America; and in particular, my supervisor, Dr. David Young, Department of Anthropology, University of Alberta. Without their comments and guidance this work would have been much more difficult to defend and complete. They were willing to take the risk of allowing me to craft an M.A. thesis different from the norm at the University of Alberta. Thanks.

I also wish to acknowledge my family and other members of the Paddle Prairie Metis Settlement who shared with me their memories and experiences of the two events contained in this work.

FORWARD

PEELING the layers of cultural meaning is a delicate process and a thing of beauty in the hands of a caring person. Exposing an oral culture to the scrutiny of the written page, baring meaning for all to see must be done in a thoughtful and respectful manner. This contribution from Elmer must be appreciated within this context.

Insight into the Metis worldview is a topic that is rarely if at all handled from an insider's perspective. Elmer originally examined this topic in his Masters' studies. I have been privileged to use this material in a number of university courses. I really appreciate his sharing the concept of gifting that is not well understood nor articulated. The information delves into the natural cycles of Metis life and places it in a context of connection to the land. Placing it in a personal context strengthens the experience for the reader and makes it that much more meaningful.

The significance of this work is that it speaks to the heart of the reader. It is about a way of life and way of living life that is quickly changing. Economic development is critical to Aboriginal communities in this fast-paced world. This work asks the question at what cost is this development. This leads to the question of what kind of communities are we working to build? These are not easy questions but if they are not asked then we will lose traditions and cultural practices without a second thought.

Ekosi,

Dr. Wanda Wuttunee
Acting Head, Native Studies
University of Manitoba

CHAPTER ONE: INTRODUCTION AND HISTORY OF PADDLE PRAIRIE

INTRODUCTION

I was fortunate enough to be born only eight years after my family moved, in the spring of 1939, onto the land set aside by the *Metis Population Betterment Act* of 1938 for the creation of a Metis Settlement at Paddle Prairie, Alberta. Under this Alberta provincial legislation, only Metis could become members of the Settlement and make a living there. My father and mother were among the first settlers to help establish the community.

My father's first language was Cree, which he could also write. My mother's first language was English. Although my father usually spoke to me and my siblings in Cree, he did have a good command of both spoken and written English. I grew up speaking both languages. My parents' knowledge was a blend of traditional and Western concepts, which was referred to as the "Metis way of doing things." From this knowledge they derived my family's livelihood, which consisted of mixed farming, raising both domesticated plants and animals, and gathering and harvesting wild plants and animals.

I was educated inside the community from grade one to grade nine. My peer group and classmates were all Metis. However, to continue my education from grade ten to post-secondary levels, I had to leave the Metis community.

From grade ten to grade twelve I attended high school in the town of Fairview, Alberta. After upgrading some grade twelve subjects at Alberta College in Edmonton, I attended the Northern Alberta Institute of Technology from 1966 to 1968, graduating with a diploma in Civil Engineering Technology. After being employed as a civil engineering technologist in the Yukon Territory and British Columbia and touring thirteen countries in Europe, I returned to my home community in 1974. The reasons for my homecoming were to become reacquainted with my parents and to take up the opportunity to work the family farm.

Upon my return, I immediately become involved in community politics. I was elected to serve as a member and chairman on the Settlement Council for a three-year term of office. My return coincided with the exploration and development of a natural gas field, in the Blue Sky Formation of northwestern Alberta. In the winter of 1974-75, I was employed by a multinational oil company as an assistant gas field construction supervisor at Keg River. The multinational oil company and other companies decided the following winter to extend their winter drilling programs onto the Settlement.

I became involved in this project as a local contractor, hired to construct right-of-way accesses and prepare wellsite locations. It was during this stage of my life that I witnessed and experienced firsthand the impact of non-renewable resource development on a sustainable livelihood.

This study is my attempt to understand the dynamics and impact of that shift in livelihood upon both my community and my life. It also addresses certain problems and issues unique to work done by an insider, which cultural anthropologists do not normally experience in collecting data in the field.

METHODOLOGY

ONE methodology of cultural anthropology is to become a participant observer in the culture of study. The anthropologist begins with a question about the culture and undertakes a comparative analysis of the culture of study within the context of the anthropologist's own culture, all the while attempting to "see" reality through the eyes of the people. Most anthropologists, in a sense, are working their way from the outside to the inside of a culture, trying to put together some more or less meaningful "pieces of knowledge." I, on the other hand, am moving in the opposite direction. I am not trying to expand my knowledge *per se*. Rather, I wish to simplify for the reader something that is very complex and personally meaningful. To achieve this in a manner that incorporates the "Metis way of doing things," I had to become quite creative.

I refer to the plan that emerged from my drawing board as "a participant's reflections about a shift in livelihood." This shift is expressed by narrating events that occurred within comparable one-year segments from two separate time periods. This plan allowed me to perform a comparative systems analysis. Some key words in the narrative are written in Cree, placed in parentheses, and italicized, to emphasize the difficulty of translating and interpreting local traditional concepts into English.

OUTLINE OF MY NARRATIVE

MY reflections and recollections are presented as demonstrating two patterns. I describe two livelihoods and the respective worldviews that they reflect through their seasonal round of activities. Interwoven with my narrative are descriptions of their modes of production. The worldview described is my own. My perspective of the universe is strongly influenced by the local traditional ecological knowledge, which was taught to me by my parents and elders with the community. It is but one individual's interpretation of Metis cosmology, which I am willing to take the risk of presenting as written narrative. Thus, my insights may conflict with those of other members of the community.

Chapter 2 narrates events of the year 1960. It begins with a description of the basic concepts of the local traditional worldview. A central concept is of a force referred to as "The Great Spirit." The Great Spirit created other spirits, a three-world universe, and living beings gifted with a spirit, mind, emotion, and body. Living beings include plants and animals. They are considered as gifts from The Great Spirit to this world we called "Land."

Metis view themselves as part of the land of living beings, and their relationships with other living beings include exchanging all their "aspects." Aspects of the spirit, mind, and emotion are thought to provide life for the body through the activities of ceremony, ritual, and sacrifice. These activities are referred to as "Spirit Gifting" when one makes a living with the land, using the gifts of plants and animals for food and medicinal purposes.

This worldview and a cosmological calendar patterned the livelihood of my family during 1960, the year described. Natural signs signalled when to begin and end the combined activities of planting, gathering, and harvesting both wild and domesticated plants and animals. The narrative describes a spiritual relationship created between the plants, animals, and people, through the process of making a living with the land.

Chapter 3 narrates events of the year 1976. The concept of mode of production is used to analyze a pattern of livelihood that comprised two modes: the construction of a natural gas field and grain farming (Asch, 1979). The technical and social relationships of these modes are described. The land, equipment, and labour, or forces of production, are more or less under the control of individuals from the community; the relationships, or means of production, are under the control of forces outside the community.

Chapter 4 summarizes the dynamics and impact of making a living *with* the land versus making a living *off* the land. The comparison demonstrates and discusses the absence of spiritual relationships and "Spirit Gifting" between living beings and the land in the second pattern of livelihood.

THE FOUNDING OF PADDLE PRAIRIE

IN the summer of 1938, my father, Adolphus, and his brothers, Louis and John-Felix, were homesteading at Notikewin, Alberta. They rode eighty miles north on horseback to inspect the land and propose a location to be set aside from provincial Crown lands as a Metis Settlement. They were excited about the land that they had ridden over; they had seen its beauty as a gift, and agreed that it would be a good location for a proposed Metis colony. Upon returning, my father and three other Metis men from the region hired a three-ton truck to take them to Joussard, Alberta, where they proposed their land selection at a meeting of the Ewing Commission.

The Ewing Commission was a Royal Commission of the province of Alberta established in 1934. It was to hold meetings and hearings to research the conditions of health, education, and general welfare of Alberta's Metis (Dickason, 1992:359). The Commission's final report recommended establishing Settlement areas in northern Alberta for the Metis to improve their substandard living conditions. My father's proposed land location fulfilled their requirements. It was accepted and recommended by the Commission under the terms of the *Metis Population Betterment Act of 1938*, creating the Keg River Metis Colony No. 1, later changed to the Keg River

Metis Settlement. The community was established on a section called Paddle Prairie, said to have received its name from a piece of a canoe paddle found in the trunk of a willow tree growing on the prairie.

The community of Paddle Prairie is located 480 miles north of Edmonton and forty-three miles south of High Level. It is situated on Mackenzie Highway No. 35. The Metis Settlement covers an area of 630 square miles, or 403,027 acres. Its boundaries extend from the Peace River westward thirty-five miles to the Sixth Meridian, and south to north from Township 101 to Township 104. The topography ranges from level to gently undulating. Two rivers, the Keg and the Boyer, cross the land from west to east and drain into the Peace River drainage system. The Chinchaga River also enters the southwest corner of the Settlement area before flowing north to join the Hay River system that drains into Great Slave Lake. The land has no large freshwater lakes, but has many sloughs and small bodies of water throughout. The vegetation is plentiful and is characterized by areas of boreal forest: mixed tree species of white and black spruce, trembling aspen (white poplar), balsam poplar (black poplar), birch, tamarack, and willow, interspersed with various species of plants and peat moss. Wild animals, birds, fish and insects are also plentiful; species include moose, deer, elk, black bear, timber wolf, coyote, fox, weasel, lynx, mink, martin, beaver, muskrat, goose, duck, grouse, northern pike, goldeye, walleye, pickerel, mosquitoes, black flies, sand flies, horseflies, lady bugs, and butterflies (McCully and Seaton, 1982:20).

The bedrock geology of the area is overlain by shales and sandstones of the Late Cretaceous Age (McCully and Seaton, 1982:26). The soils are mostly grey wooded with the exception of the black topsoil found in the hamlet site. Both types sustain agriculture. The climate is characterized by long, cold winters and short, warm summers. January has a mean daily temperature of -21.5°C, and July of 15.7°C. The region has an average annual rainfall of 15.87 inches and sixty-two frost-free days (McCully and Seaton, 1982:17).

Throughout 1939, Metis families moved across country, either by horse team on a wagon road or by riverboat on the Peace River, to settle at Paddle Prairie. They came from such places as Keg River, Fort Vermilion, Carcajou, North Star, Notikewin, Valleyview, Grande Prairie, Wabasca, and Grande Centre, and they numbered about seventy people.

The people elected three members to their first Settlement Council. The Council formed a local government system that could approve membership and land allocations pursuant to the regulations of the *Metis Population Betterment Act*. My father was chosen as their chairman and leader. The first area to be settled and developed into a hamlet was the prairie, on surveyed parcels of land that ranged in size from eighty to 160 acres. The population continued to increase over the years through a steady birthrate and in-migration of new members. By 1960, the population had grown to 260 people, and by 1976, it had increased to 360 people. These first settlers made a living with the land. They desired to create their own happy and healthy community, thus securing a good future for their children.

CHAPTER TWO: LIVING WITH THE LAND

BASIC CONCEPTS OF THE METIS WORLDVIEW

THE local traditional Metis worldview, which my father and mother taught to me, is of a living universe (*misiwe uske*). My father's lessons were totally in the Cree language, which might indicate that he had more of a Cree cultural perspective on life than my mother, whose lessons were mostly in the English language. They taught me that *misiwe uske* comprises three worlds, which are blended together one on top of the other. These worlds are referred to as the spirit world (*kechi uske*), this world (*oma uske*), and the evil world (*muchi uske*). The living universe was created by an entity referred to as "The Great Spirit" (*Kechi Manitow*). The Great Spirit then created other spirits (*achahkwak*) to help provide harmony and balance to the universe. These spirits include Our Father (*Nohtawenan*), Our Mother (*Kikawenan*), Our Grandfathers (*Omoshomimawak*), and Our Grandmothers (*Okohkomimawak*). They were gifted with spiritual power to transform or shift shape into different forms. Spirit messengers (*powagunak*), who may appear in dreams (*pawatumowina*) as male or female, were also gifted with powers to transform or shift shape into different forms of spiritual (good) and evil (bad) forces.

Dream spirits bring a gift of life. The gift contains the aspects of the spirit (*achahk*), the mind (*mamitoneyichikun*), and emotion (*moosetawin*), brought from the spirit world. They complement the aspect of the body (*meyaw*), which was created by The Great Spirit from the elements of this world now referred to as Mother Earth. These creations, or living beings, were created simultaneously, both males and females. They include plants and animals, including insects, and all other elements of Mother Earth. Living beings have a life cycle of birth and death, and have good and bad forces. They are interdependent and equal to one another. Human beings (*ayiseniwak*) were created as one of the animal species of living beings.

The challenge for Metis people is to keep their aspects of the spirit, mind, emotion, and body in harmony and balance. Balance of good and bad forces, both within each person and in the universe, must be achieved if people wish to sustain and live a happy and healthy life. Food to sustain life is created by The Great Spirit. It comes in the form of a gift (*mekiwin*), or something that is freely exchanged and shared between a donor and recipient through the relationships of giving and receiving.

Different forms of food, in sets of good and bad, are required for the different aspects. The source of food for the aspect of the body is Mother Earth. The food for the aspects of the mind, emotion, and spirit is obtained from all three worlds. Food for the body consists of gifts in the form of the elements of air, water, meat, fruit, and grains. Food for the mind consists of gifts of experience and knowledge, and comes in the form of creating, thinking, learning, and teaching. Food for the emotion consists of gifts, which come in the form of love, happiness, anger, and pain. Food for the spirit consists of gifts of spirituality, both good and bad, and comes in the form of giving, receiving, sharing, stealing, hoarding, and greediness.

One acquires these gifts through the activities of ceremony (*wuskawewin*), ritual (*isehchikewin*), and sacrifice (*kamekith-kmiteochi*). Ceremony is the physical movement of the aspect of the body performed by the Metis in order to make a living. Ritual is the repeated patterns of Metis behaviour, created by ideas, beliefs, values, feelings, etc., using the aspects of their mind and emotion, in order to make a living. Sacrifice is the offering and requesting of life (from the heart) from a plant or animal by the Metis in order to continue living.

These activities are accomplished, within a Metis livelihood, through a series of continuous relationships established by gift exchanges with plants and animals. Metis procreation is accomplished sharing the entire aspects of the spirit, mind, emotion, and body between a man and woman. It is the same for the male and female species of plants and other animals. The spirit, mind, and emotion are the only constant aspects in gift exchanges between any combination of living beings, and this exchange is referred to as "Spirit Gifting" (*Mekia-chahkwewin*).

Gifts are considered by the Metis to be the intangible and tangible forms of the aspects of mind, emotion, spirit, and body exchanged in a relationship between a donor and a recipient. A gift without the spiritual aspect of its donor is not considered a gift by its recipient. The greatest gift (*kechi mekiwin*) to the Metis is life, symbolized by the heart, because life came to this world at the birth of living beings in the everlasting aspects of the spirit, mind, and emotion from the spirit world. The body will decompose back to the elements of Mother Earth upon the death of an individual and the spirit, mind, and emotion, or its life, will return to the spirit world.

Sacrifice, giving, and receiving from the heart, is the rite of separation of any of the aspects of the spirit, mind, and emotion from the aspect of the body through Spirit Gifting. Some members of the Paddle Prairie community initiated Spirit Gifting through ceremony and ritual. A ceremony is the Metis pattern of lived performance. It is the gathering and harvesting of plants and animals in order to make a living with the land. In this livelihood, a ritual is considered to be a decision made through the recital of a prayer by a gatherer or harvester. The person requests permission from The Great Spirit, Mother Earth, and the aspects of the spirit, mind, and emotion of a plant or animal to sacrifice its aspect of the body for human sustenance. The spirits of the donor and recipient are thought to be equal. This request is in exchange for an offering in the form of a gift of a pinch of tobacco or food, and it signals spiritual equality. The activities of sacrifice and ritual are considered to be performed in a border region, which overlaps and joins the different worlds. This allows access to the spiritual and evil forces of the spirit world and the evil world to this world. The gatherer or harvester performing the acts of praying, singing, drumming, dancing, and burning a diamond willow fungus or tobacco can open a pathway between this world and the spirit world. The path forms a gateway through which messages and spiritual forces are communicated back and forth. The performer must have experience and knowledge of the good and bad messages of spiritual forces in order to distinguish their differences. Only then can he or she can access and use them for good or bad needs.

The evil world (*muchi uske*), created by The Great Spirit, is inhabited by The Evil Spirit (*Muchi Manitow*) and its evil spirit helpers (*muchi powagunak*). They upset harmony and balance in this world. They fight The Great Spirit and good spirits for control of the aspects of the mind, emotion, and spirit of Metis people. Evil spirits have the ability to transform and shift shape into any of the aspects of plants and animals or the gifts of food used by the Metis in this world. Upon this transformation, they can implant more bad forces into a Metis and upset his or her harmony and balance. The daily challenge for Metis is to maintain a balanced set of good and bad forces of the aspects of body, mind, emotion, and spirit in making a living with the land. An imbalance of these aspects can lead to a Metis' having an unhappy and unhealthy life.

THE SEASONS OF THE METIS

IN 1960, my family used the preceding sacred worldview and the following Metis cosmological calendar to pattern their livelihood. Natural signs signalled when to begin and end a seasonal round of activities of cleaning the land, planting, and gathering and harvesting both wild and domesticated plants and animals.

Niski Pesim or Goose Moon

In bush Metis (*Sakaw Ayiseniwak*) local traditional ecological knowledge (*kayas ochi kake pe itotumik kiske yitumowin*), there is a phrase in Cree (*Nehiyawewin*), *niski pesim*, which translates into English as "goose moon." It is the time in a one-year cycle of Mother Earth at the community of Paddle Prairie when geese (*niska*) are first sighted on their spring migratory flight. They travel from the south (*sawunohk*) to their spring nesting grounds in the north (*kewetinohk*). In the Gregorian calendar, goose moon is called March. The arrival of geese signals to the Metis that spring (*sekwun*) has come.

In a late spring, snow has not started to thaw when the geese arrive. In an early spring, a warm wind blowing from the west (*pahkisimotahk*) to the east (*sakastenohk*) has already melted the snow, forming pools of water in low areas of farm fields and sloughs. Within days of the geese's arrival, other waterfowl and summer birds arrive. This begins the Metis life cycle (*ohipiwin*) activity of making a livelihood (*pimachisiwin*) with the land. The cycle's commencement is observed through the ceremony of eating a bowl of duck soup (*sesep mechimapoy*) and making spring fires (*sekwuna suskwuna*).

Where the winter snow has thawed and melted, spring fires are used to start the process of cleaning (*kunachitawiwin*) the land. Snow melts first around buildings, such as the family house, chicken coop, storage sheds, and granaries, where the sun has reflected heat waves off the walls onto the grass. The buildings are in no danger of catching on fire (*iskotew*) because the ground is wet and the amount of dried grasses is insufficient to cause flame hot enough to burn wood. A wet gunnysack and a pail of water also stand by for emergencies. As the sun's heat continues to melt the snow and exposes patches of dead dried grasses in the farm fields and hay meadows, those patches are also fired.

Firing was performed by my older brothers. They walked side by side in a line, with their backs to the wind using fire torches to ignite the grass. Their torches were made from a twist of dried grass or a cloth soaked with kerosene and tied on the end of a stick. A light touch of their torches would ignite the patches of exposed grass, creating what looked like a broken line of fire burning away from my brothers. My father's role was to act as the fire supervisor. I acted as a rear fireguard, extinguishing any late flare-ups near the buildings. Our old dog, Bunch, assisted me in keeping a lookout for these spot fires.

Snow does not melt evenly during the spring thaw cycle. It is thus impossible to fire fall cereal grain stubble, straw in farm fields, and dead grasses in hay meadows all at the same time. This creates a pattern of burnt and unburnt patches over the land. As the melting snow recedes into the bush, it uncovers patches of dead trees (*metosak*) and grass, which are then fired. Live, dormant trees are too wet and green to burn, and so the process of firing does not harm them. Metis spring firing cleans and clears areas of prairie, slough meadows, fields, and brush of debris. This makes it possible for new grasses and trees to grow again. Firing acts not only as a fireguard around communities during the forest fire season, but also as a method of forest maintenance. It ensures that making a livelihood with the land will continue into the future.

Ayeki Pesim or Frog Moon

Spring firing could last well into *ayeki pesim,* "frog moon," or the month of April. This is the month when frogs reappear from winter hibernation. We were alerted to their presence by a twenty-four-hour mating ritual, which consisted of a continuous croaking chorus in the creek and slough near our house.

The months of March and April brought other forms of life to the land, including newborn farm animals. My father raised cattle, horses, hogs, and chickens. Unlike horses and hogs, cattle have trouble giving birth. The calving operation had to be closely monitored, as cattle sometimes like to wander off from the herd to give birth. As the calf is born delicate and helpless, it might otherwise easily freeze to death.

The swollen stomach and udder of a cow are the first telltale signs that she will give birth within the month. My family would partition off a portion of the barn and bed it with a foot of straw. The cow would be penned there until she gave birth. A day before her delivery began, milk would drip from her udder and she would become restless. Calves were usually born during the night. We would check on the cows every two hours, around the clock, ready to assist any cows experiencing labour difficulties. It was exciting when a calf was finally born and had its first suckle of birthing milk. This milk was thick, rich and deep yellow in colour. My mother would use it to make a raisin and bread pudding to celebrate the birth. It was one of my favourite desserts.

This season's beginning was marked by my mother planting garden seeds. She placed them in bedding soil packed into tin cans, and lined them in rows on window sills to catch sunlight. Samples of seeds to be used for spring planting were blessed at a special Roman Catholic High Mass. We recited Cree prayers at home, asking for their successful germination, fruitfulness, and protection from a late spring frost.

Pininawawe Pesim or Egg-Laying Moon

When Pininawawe pesim ("egg-laying moon" or the month of May) arrived, my mother's bedding plants were ready to be transplanted into the garden plot prepared by my father. He did all the cultivation of our farmland using horses and horse-drawn farm equipment. My father would begin the spring field work by plowing the land with a two-bottom plow, drawn by four workhorses who were hitched side by side. This operation turned over the soil to a depth of six inches in strips measuring eighteen inches wide. He usually began work at 7:00 a.m. and finished at 6:00 p.m. At 10:00 a.m. and 3:00 p.m., my father would give the horses a rest and some water and oats. At noon he stopped for an hour's rest, again feeding and watering the horses. My father always cared for the horses before allowing himself rest or food.

When the plowing operation was completed, the soil was disked to loosen it and break it down into small chunks. Harrowing, floating, and smoothing the land would make a seed-bed ready for seeding. My mother would begin to plant her vegetable seeds and transplant the seedlings in the newly worked garden bed sometime after the middle of May. It would be a time when the soil was sufficiently warmed, the last threatening frost had passed, and it was the beginning of the full moon.

My mother would begin the planting process by raking the garden bed free of any unbroken lumps of soil and dead roots. She would mark the first row to be planted, using a line of string as a guide. She would make two furrows by pulling a wooden tool through the earth. She poured water into the furrows to dampen the soil, ensuring that the seeds would have enough moisture to germinate and begin growing. Each seed was hand-planted in the prepared rows, two inches apart and two inches deep, and then covered and tamped. My mother planted a variety of vegetable seeds in this manner, including carrots, peas, radishes, onions, lettuce, cabbage, beans, turnips, pumpkin, cucumber, and corn.

The tiny, delicate plants would begin to sprout from the soil within two weeks from the time of planting. Along with the plants came many different species of local plants, "weeds," that were removed because they competed for the same water and nutrients as the vegetables. These plants were hand-pulled or hoed between the rows and fed to the hogs. Normal rain was sufficient for the garden; but during a dry spell, water from the creek had to be hauled by buckets.

Planting potatoes required a different method from that used to plant the smaller garden seeds: this was an operation undertaken by my father and my older brothers. Seed potatoes were chosen from the potato bin in the dirt cellar of our house. These potatoes were cut in quarters, which we ensured each had a potato eye. We left them to dry in the sunlight for two days before planting them. A furrow was made four to six inches in depth by a one-bottom walking plow pulled by Barney, our gentle Cayuse workhorse. The seed potatoes, carried in a five-gallon pail, were planted eighteen inches apart and covered by the soil that the plowshare turned over making the next furrow. The potato garden was seeded in three-foot-wide rows in a one-acre plot. A horse-drawn cultivator weeded this area; in the process, it banked soil onto the growing tuberous plants. As planting of the potato garden was usually completed in one day, it did not disrupt the planting of the farm's cereal grains.

My father's cereal crops consisted of the early, northern ninety-day species of wheat, barley, and oats. Prior to planting, they were cleaned and treated for smut, a rust fungus. The grains were cleaned of weeds and chaff by passing them through a hand-cranked fanning mill. Seeds were placed in a hopper located on top of the fanning mill and sifted through a series of different-sized screens. A fan blew air through them as they rolled down the screens, removing the chaff, and the smaller weed seeds fell through the screens into a bucket and were fed to our hogs. Fanning grain was a slow, time-consuming pro-cess. Seeds were planted using a horse-drawn twelve-foot seed drill. Preparation of the fields began when enough moisture had evaporated to allow the workhorses to walk on the soil without sinking beyond a depth of four inches. This operation was completed by the third week in May, near the time when my mother and Old Lady Margaret would begin sapping birch trees, as the sap was at its maximum flow.

My role was to assist my mother and Old Lady Margaret. Old Lady Margaret was also my aunt, the wife of my father's brother. I remember how the .22-calibre rabbit gun and back-pack I was carrying that year seemed to get heavier as we traveled further and further into the bush. In 1960 I was chosen for the first time to be a protector from black bears and timber wolves; hence the rabbit gun – but my mother kept the shells.

As my excitement in my new status lessened, I realized that I should not have agreed so readily with my mother to pack my backpack so heavily. I also realized that the gun was really a decoy: their hidden purpose was for me to carry the food, water, tin cans, knife, and axe to be used to collect the sap. My thoughts of shooting a black bear were replaced by thoughts of the weight of the heavy backpack. It seemed to take forever before my aunt finally decided that we had reached the place to start tapping birch trees.

She began by making a small fire of dead grasses, dead willow branches, and dried diamond willow fungus. Once the fire had caught and the flames were burning with sufficient force, she threw a pinch of tobacco and some food into the fire and said a Metis prayer. The smoke would purify, making a mediating bridge between this world and the spirit world, and communicating the prayer and spiritual forces back and forth between the two worlds. The smoke would be smelled by others in the vicinity, a signal to them that this place was being used for the time. The prayer she said was:

Nohtawenan, Kechi desikohk kayayan, ki mawimostatin asumemea, mena Kikawenan ekwa omuskeke kechi mekiwina. Muskeke tomeyo totakot awa ka ahosit. Hiy, Hiy, kinanaskomitin. Pitane ekosi teyekhi.

Our Father Spirit of the heavens, I beg of you and Our Mother and her great gifts of medicine. This medicine will do good for those who have come to me for healing. Always being ever so thankful. This is all for now.

The prayer over, my aunt served food and tea to my mother and me. It was about 10:00 a.m. The sun's power was strong enough to begin the cycle of life for daytime living beings, signalled both by the morning's dew having evaporated and my noticing that my moosehide moccasins had become dry.

My aunt began selecting live birch trees to sap. She chose trees at least six inches in diameter, and marked them by tying a string of red yarn around their trunks about four feet above the ground. She then made a tobacco offering by the base of each tree. I counted twelve trees in total. During my aunt's activity, my mother was preparing green willow pegs one inch in diameter and eight inches long. I observed that before my mother would cut a live willow branch, she would also make a tobacco offering to the willow tree. My job was to skin the bark off the pegs and take them to my aunt. The bark peeled easily because the sap was running.

Once my aunt had finished selecting the birch trees to be sapped, she began the tapping process by inserting a willow peg under the bark of each tree at the place on the trunk where she had tied the red yarn. She made a small cut into the bark to the depth of the wood, then lifted the bark with the tip of the knife blade, and inserted the smooth, peeled willow peg at a forty-five-degree angle sloping downward from the tree trunk. The small cut would later heal and not kill the birch tree. My mother, right behind us, was tying a tin can the size of a quart jar to the tree trunk just below the willow peg so that it caught the dripping sap. Within a few minutes, I could hear the drip, drip, drip, of the sap into the cans.

I remember that it was now about noon, because the sun was directly overhead. My aunt decided it was time to have lunch and drink some tea. I observed that my aunt and my mother had not spoken a word of English since they had left home. All conversations had taken place in Cree, and I understood the words and their meanings. Just before we left for home, my aunt gave me a taste of the sap. It tasted a little bitter, but the offer made me feel important, so I thanked her. She told me that on our way home we would set some rabbit snares.

True to my aunt's word, we stopped at a site where my father and uncle had made a spring fire five years before to clean old dead willows, poplars and grasses. This cleaning would allow young tender willows and white poplar trees to grow, which rabbits would feed upon. Close to the new growth was a thick stand of spruce trees and deadfall that provided cover and shelter for small animals. My aunt located the main rabbit run and set two brass wire snares four inches in diameter. She placed them six inches off the ground and twenty feet apart. We marked the spot by bending branches over them. It was then that I realized I was committed to coming back the next day to check the snares.

I was anxious to return to the sapping site and the snares. Time seemed to pass very slowly. My aunt had made the activities so interesting and exciting that I did not think of it as work at all. It was unlike my usual daily work of sawing and chopping firewood for my mother's wood cook stove, which I still had to do upon returning home. The next day our sapping group left at about 8:00 a.m. to collect the sap.

My mother told me that in the old days they would make camp at the sapping site for one or two weeks. Sapping time was viewed as a holiday and a time for the women to get together and socialize. The groups consisted of grandmothers, aunts, mothers, daughters, and granddaughters from various kin groups in the community. The fathers would drive the group out to the site with a team of horses and return to pick them up at a later date. The group was left with one old experienced bush horse and some dogs for travel and protection in the case of an emergency.

On our return to the sapping site, my aunt stopped at the location where she had set the rabbit snares. It was the moment that occurred over and over again in my dream that night, but from my dream I could not remember if a rabbit had been caught or not. My aunt asked me to check the snares, and my heart pounded in my chest. It was the moment of truth, and to my surprise both snares had caught a rabbit. I came out of the willow and poplar bluff holding the dead rabbits by their back legs high in front of me so that both my mother and aunt could see the catch. In my mind I took credit for the catch because I had checked the snares. My aunt then instructed me to take a pinch of tobacco and offer it to Our Mother and the rabbit spirits, because the rabbits had sacrificed their lives so that their bodies could be eaten as food by people.

My aunt expertly skinned and gutted the rabbits without using a knife. She first broke the rabbit skin with her fingers between each pair of legs and above each hind leg. She then pulled the skin inside out from the hind legs to the head and disconnected the skin at the ears and nose. She tore a small incision with her fingers into the rabbit's stomach above where the hind legs are joined, through which she gutted the internal organs, saving the spiritual gifts of the heart and liver of each rabbit. Before my aunt had finished skinning and cleaning the rabbits, I could taste the rabbit stew my mother would make for supper that evening. The whole operation took ten minutes or less. Then we continued on to the sapping site.

When we reached the sapping site, I ran around to each birch tree to check the amount of sap that had collected in the tin cans. Some cans were half full, and others were full to the brim. None had spilt over. My aunt had timed our return so that no sap would be wasted. The total amount collected that first day was two and a half gallons, which became the average daily volume collected over the entire two-week sapping period. I observed my aunt would select a new birch tree to replace the ones that did not yield as much as the others, and offered a pinch of tobacco by each newly chosen tree.

On our way home, my aunt reset the rabbit snares. Our travel party rested more often now, because our backpacks were much heavier loaded with the sap. I still carried the .22 rifle. I did not know whether or not a black bear would suddenly appear out of nowhere, but in my mind, guns gave a person a sense of protection from the unknown. I came to understand much later that the real protection from black bears and the unknown was my aunt's and mother's ecological knowledge of the natural instincts of black bears and the spirit world.

Upon our return home, my first instruction was to take a gallon of sap to the water well and hang it just above the surface of the cold water. Our drinking water well was dug to the level of the water table, about fifteen feet below the surface of the ground. The well had a wooden cribbing and a hand-cranked wooden cylinder with a sisal rope tied to it, which was used to lower and raise the water bucket and other buckets containing butter, milk, and meat to keep them cool and fresh. The water well served as our summer refrigerator. During the summer months, my mother would ask me to go and fetch the sap so my parents could drink a cup of it whenever they were not feeling well. At that time, I could not understand why the bitter-tasting liquid would make my parents feel better.

My mother would start making syrup from the sap by boiling it in a gallon pot on the wood cook stove. She would keep the sap boiling until she felt that enough water had evaporated. She then added other ingredients, such as sugar, flour, and dried saskatoon berries, which would make it into a sweet-tasting syrup. My mother would pour the syrup into glass jars, let it cool, screw on old covers, and store it on the canning shelves in the dirt cellar of our house.

The syrup was used as a spread on bannock, bread, and pancakes during the winter months of December, January, and February. Any remaining syrup was saved for the following winter months. My mother informed me that the reason the syrup was used only during those months was that the sun was then at its weakest strength and could not supply enough sunlight to keep us healthy. The birch tree sap syrup and spirit would keep us from becoming unbalanced and unhealthy at this time of the year.

My father had other experiences and knowledge about the properties of the birch trees. He told me that the birch tree's spirit and bark had healing properties to cure skin wounds and disease. The surface and inner bark were used as a poultice to draw out infections. The inner bark was scraped off the hard wood surface, and then applied to the infected area on the skin. The area would then be covered with the soft, paper-thin outer bark, and wrapped with a cloth to hold it in place over the infected area. My mother treated me for an infected axe wound on my right leg, from which I still bear a scar, with this healing practice. She also made a cast from the hard birch bark to cover the wound, to protect it from being disturbed during the healing process.

My father informed me that birch had very strong tensile and compressive strengths, and compared favourably in uses to hardwoods such as oak and maple. He used birch wood to make and repair various broken wooden parts of farm machinery. My father also made me my first bow from the dried branch of a tree. He selected a branch naturally shaped as a bow and carved it with his pocket knife. The bow had excellent resiliency and would spring back into its original shape upon the release of the bow string. My arrows were made from saskatoon tree shafts, with blunt tips and chicken feathers for guidance at the ends. My father instructed me never to shoot arrows at a person or directly overhead, because on their downward flight they could accidentally strike me.

The month of May transformed our environment into a sea of green, teeming with young native plants and animals. As the spring sun warmed the water in the creek and slough, it hatched the first batch of bloodsucking insects: mosquitoes, sand flies, blackflies, and horseflies. We made a smoke insect repellent by smudging: making a smouldering fire that caused great amounts of smoke. We made ours with wood chips in an old galvanized water pail to which we added green grass. The smudge pail was kept by the main door of our house, where its smoke kept insects from entering. A larger smudge was made for the livestock.

This animal smudge was made in a fenced fire pit in the barnyard. The fence kept the livestock from walking into the burning material and harming themselves. A fire was made using dry and green wood for fuel; we then covered it with horse manure, causing it to make smoke. If the smudge was properly made, it usually burned until the next morning at which time it had to be remade. The seasonal cycle for mosquitoes and flies began in mid-May and lasted until the first week in August.

Paskawe Pesim or Egg-Hatching Moon

The end of May brought in *paskawe pesim*, "egg-hatching moon," or the month of June. June was the time of year when bird's eggs hatched at Paddle Prairie. Many different species of ducks and summer birds nested in the willow thickets, saskatoon and chokecherry bushes, and black and white poplar trees along the banks of the creek running through our property. The most common ducks were the mallard and the small teal, and common summer birds were robins, blackbirds, sparrows, crows, and hawks.

I remember one day in the first week of June when my younger brother came running excitedly into the house because he had discovered a robin's nest and seen a baby robin, which looked like a feather. It was his first experience of finding a bird's nest.

Finding the most duck and summer bird's nests was a game I played with my younger brother and older sister. A robin's nest was the least difficult to find, and a blackbird's nest the most difficult. Blackbirds make their nests in locations that blend into the environment. We found them by studying the bird's flight paths and roosts. My mother told us never to breathe onto the nests or touch the baby birds because their parents could abandon them.

June was the month of the most sunlight and the time to repair the house, farm buildings, and fences. I grew up in a two-story frame house constructed by my father and my older brothers in 1946. Its walls, built on two-foot tamarack footings over a dirt storage cellar, were insulated with wood shavings. It had windows with single glass panes. On the main floor were the porch, dining room, kitchen, washroom, water barrel, wood box, living room, wood cook stove, wood heater, recreation living room, and my parents' bedroom. On the second floor were the family bedrooms and a recreation area. A kerosene gas lamp, a table lamp, and a lantern provided lighting after the daylight hours. Underneath the stairway leading to the second floor was a storage closet. Over the main door was a gun rack containing all of my father's hunting rifles, .22s, shotguns, and cleaning rods. He kept the gun shells in his bedroom. The gun rack was built at such a height that it was impossible for us children to reach it until we grew old enough to use them. My father was a gifted hunter, trapper, and farmer, and we respected his guns.

We did all of the necessary repairs for our home ourselves. For example, one year my older brothers re-shingled the roof on our house. This was a big task, because the house had walls sixteen feet high. They had to construct a special scaffolding to access the roof, pry off the old rotten wood shingles, and replace them with new Domtar asphalt shingles. Another time, they built a new hog barn with ten furrowing stalls. That year my father raised 250 hogs and established a community record. Raising that many hogs required planning and hard work.

Hogs are a difficult farm animal to keep penned. Fences have to be well-constructed and continually repaired. Old fence posts and rails were replaced with new diamond willow posts and spruce rails that were cut when the sap was running. The hogs were fed a ration of crushed oats, watered three times a day, and had their pens cleaned and bedded with new straw daily. When they reached an average weight of 250 pounds they were shipped by hired truck, along with wheat and cattle, to a market at Grimshaw, 140 miles to the south.

Other fences and buildings were repaired during this time as well. Old barbed wire, rotten and broken fence posts and rails were dismantled and then replaced on the fences that surrounded the fields and made up the barnyard corrals and feedlot. Leaking roofs and broken door hinges were repaired or replaced if necessary. Any broken parts on the farm machinery used for the spring field work were repaired by the blacksmith at the community iron forge. Maintenance of the farm buildings and equipment was completed by the end of June and early July.

Pusko Pesim or Molting Moon

Pusko Pesim, or "Moulting Moon," is the month of July. It is the time of year when the adult ducks molt their old feathers and grow new ones. During this process they cannot fly. When this cycle begins, it also signals to my father that the slough hay has matured enough to be harvested as feed for our livestock. My father's natural grass hay meadow was located about ten miles from the farm, along the wagon road to the Peace River. The distance was too far for him and my older brothers to come home every day after haying, so it was necessary to make a hay camp. They had to live in a canvas tent at the hay meadow for a period of two to three weeks beginning in the middle of July. When I reached the age of thirteen, my father requested for the first time that I come along to learn the traditional ecological knowledge and help with the work.

My first task was to help with preparing the food and tools that would be required for making hay. We carefully loaded the wagon box with a variety of foods packed into our grub box, such as flour, sugar, tea, salt, baking powder, potatoes, carrots, turnips, canned milk, canned wild berries, and drinking water. These foods would be cooked with wild meats harvested at the campsite and constituted the basis of our diet. Tools included wrenches, haywire, pliers, an axe, a saw, a hammer, nails, a water pail, bedrolls, a change of clothing, a six-man canvas tent, and wooden matches. Two gunny sacks of oats weighing 100 pounds each were loaded as feed for the horses.

I remember checking the horse harness for breaks and mending any broken leather straps with copper rivets. My father brought out the hay mower from storage. He prepared it by checking the moving parts such as the pitman arm, cutting sickle, knife guards and the bullgear dogs to ensure they were in good working order. To operate the hay mower, you first had to put it in gear, lower the cutting bar to a level of four inches above the ground, and then pull it with the team of horses. The pulling engaged the gears that put the cutting sickle into operation. This cut an eight-foot swath of slough hay through the meadow and in the process created a loud noise of moving parts. When all preparations were completed to my father's satisfaction, we set out to the hay meadow.

I drove the team of horses, Barney and May, who pulled the loaded wagon with our supplies. Tied to the back of the wagon box was my saddle horse, Diamond. My father drove the extra team of horses, Dapple and Best, pulling the hay mower. I learned to drive a team of horses and hitch them to a wagon all by myself. My father trained the old team of horses that I drove to stop on the command of "whoa" and to begin again on the command of "giddy up." Barney and May were our most reliable team, and my father did not have to worry about them running away on me. It took us about three hours to reach the campsite at the hay meadow. We immediately pitched the canvas tent on the same location as last year, using the same tent poles. While I was unloading our supplies from the wagon, my father began to cut hay in the meadow. He made the first swath counter clockwise, to make a path, and thereafter all the swaths were clockwise. My next chore was to cook our supper. After super my father usually spoke of our local traditional worldview, while we sat around the campfire drinking tea. After this spiritual lesson was over for the day, he would instruct me to go and harvest a duck for the next day's meal and practice the knowledge of the lesson in order to acquire the experience of a bush Metis of making a living with the land.

Located near our campsite was a large slough that beavers had made by damming a creek. Water had flooded a low area, transforming it into a slough and providing an ecosystem for many different species of plants, insects, ducks, and other animals. I took a single-shot, twelve-gauge shotgun and was instructed not to load a shell into its firing chamber until I was sure of making a duck harvest. The method of duck harvesting in sloughs requires the harvester to walk in water waist high. I did not have a pair of hip waders, so I had to wade into the slough water wearing only blue jeans and sneakers. The water would initially feel cold, but within seconds my body would adapt to its temperature and I would feel warmer.

I remember one harvesting in particular that July. I slowly walked among the tall bulrushes and slough hay, while keeping a close watch for a mallard and reciting a prayer asking Our Mother to provide me with one of her gifts and asking forgiveness for harvesting a duck. While separating the reeds with the end of the shotgun barrel I came face to face with a garter snake who was also seeking food for a meal. I wonder who was more frightened, I or the snake? The snake took off like a shooting arrow skimming over the surface of the water. I slowly regained my composure before continuing on with the harvest. I spotted a flock of male mallard ducks sitting on a partially exposed log of a beaver house about 200 feet from me. A slight breeze was blowing from them towards me so they had not caught my scent or heard my movements. The shotgun made a booming noise and the slough became extremely quiet; one lifeless duck remained near the log.

On the way back to the campsite, I made an offering of a piece of bannock as a gift to Our Mother and the duck's spirit in exchange for sacrificing its body for our food. With this ritual completed, I began to pluck its feathers and had cleaned the body by the time I returned to camp. My father showed me how to prepare the duck's meat for food. We stripped the intestines of water, digested grasses, and insects, draped them over a stick, and cooked them over the hot coals of the campfire. They were the first to be eaten. They had a sweet taste and were delicious to a hungry boy. The heart and liver were boiled with the rest of the meat to make a soup. The remaining internal organs and feet were discarded to be eaten by other animals. After this activity was completed, we retired for the night and recited evening prayers. I was completely exhausted by the day's work, and by the time my head hit my pillow, I was fast asleep.

We arose every morning at 6:00 and while my father cooked bacon and eggs for breakfast, my chore was to water, feed, and groom the horses. I watered the teams by riding one horse and leading the other by its halter shank to the creek. Their feed was a gallon each of oats and all the slough hay they could eat. The hay was stacked into an outdoor manger and double stall constructed of diamond willows. I also had to remake the smudge fire before being allowed to eat.

After breakfast was completed, my father would check the hay mower machine for loose bolts and grease its moving parts. When the night's dew had been evaporated by the sun's heat waves, I would harness the team and my father would begin cutting hay. I was kept busy while my father was working by washing the dishes, tidying the camp, preparing meals, and harvesting ducks. I would also ride my saddle horse back to the farm for supplies.

I taught myself to ride a horse at a young age. I could ride bareback extremely well, and my father considered me a good horseman by the time I was thirteen. My father, in the past, had had a stallion and brood mares that he used for raising our workhorses. He continually taught me about horses. His method of training horses consisted of pressure, release, and reward. I was told never to tie a rope that was connected to a horse, such as a halter shank or bridle, to any part of my body, and never to get into a situation where I could lose control to the horse. He firmly believed that a trainer could communicate mental, physical, and spiritual instructions that a horse could understand and respond to. This knowledge about horses allowed me to halter break and ride my saddle horse, Diamond, when he was two years old. He was the horse I rode back and forth to the farm for supplies. Riding bareback, I carried fresh bannock, potatoes, bacon, etc. in a backpack.

The trip to the farm from the hay camp took one and one half hours one way. If I left the camp at 10:30 a.m., I would be home in time to have lunch with my mother and the rest of the family. My mother would pack us supplies and I would return to the camp. During those trips I saw some of the bigger animals, such as moose and deer, who are not afraid of horses because horses have four legs. My father was an expert at harvesting moose, and some of his favourite stories were about this activity.

Moose are intelligent animals, and a person has to be gifted with the necessary talents in order to be a successful moose harvester. My father considered moose to be similar to other plants and animals, a gift, and harvesting them was conducted within the Metis context of ceremony, ritual, and sacrifice. He required a dream in which his dream spirit would inform him of having made contact with a moose spirit and when and where to harvest the moose. The information contained the age and sex of the moose, topography of the land, weather conditions, and the equipment required for the harvest.

On one occasion, my father's dream spirit informed him that the wind, a grandfather spirit, would assist him if he rode his bush horse, leading a packhorse, to a certain bend in the Keg River at the time of the full moon. This bend was marked by a stand of spruce trees. He was told to then make a call sounding like a two-year-old bull moose; the moose would then come to him, as it had chosen to willingly sacrifice its body for food. He was to return this gift by making an offering of tobacco, burning a diamond willow fungus and hanging the "bell," or the strip of hair that hangs down from under the moose's chin, on a tree after the sacrifice had been performed. This ritual would ensure that the spirit of the moose would make a safe journey back to the spirit world from which it had come and would not get trapped in this world.

My father faithfully followed the visions in his dreams and was successful in harvesting moose by this method. The moose were expertly prepared by my father and all parts were used. Moose meat, cooked with the vegetables from my mother's garden into a stew, was a staple part of our diet. The moose nose, tongue, large intestine, heart, liver, kidneys, and bone marrow were eaten at different times of the year. My mother preserved the meat by canning and drying it. In the winter my father hung it in our meat house to freeze dry. My mother tanned the moose hide and made it into clothing for the family, such as mittens and moccasins.

It normally took my father about two weeks to complete cutting hay in the meadow during the hay season, providing the weather remained good. After my father finished cutting the hay, we left it to be dried by the sun and wind. I would then begin to rake it into hay coils, small piles of hay, using a rake machine pulled by a team of horses. The rake machine resembled a skeleton. It was constructed with small-diameter, tubular metal pipe for lightness and had large diameter wheels on an axle three feet above the ground and a frame fourteen feet wide. After the hay was raked into windrows, my father would return to the farm, his work completed. Now my older brothers would come to the camp and stack the hay into haystacks.

My older brothers would bring along some friends to assist us. Although stacking hay in the heat of July was backbreaking work, it was lightened somewhat by our joking. Hay was stacked by pitchfork onto a ten by sixteen foot float constructed of dried white poplar rails and pulled by a four horse team. The hay float was pulled alongside the hay coils, which were forked onto it and compacted by two people trampling it down. This process was continued until either the stack of hay was the proper amount for a hayrack load, or it became too high to pitch hay up to its top. The stack was then anchored onto the ground by rails and ropes and dragged off the float to a location that could be easily accessed by a hayrack wagon team. In the evening my older brothers and friends would entertain us.

All three of my older brothers are musically gifted, and have learned to sing country music and play the guitar. One older brother learned to play the fiddle as well. Sometimes they sang solo and other times they sang in harmony. The most popular song artists at this time were Johnny Cash and Elvis Presley, and their songs "I Walk The Line," "Ring Of Fire," "Jail House Rock," and "Love Me Tender" were sung while we sat around the campfire drinking tea, telling stories and generating humour. Often we just gazed at the stars, where we were sometimes treated with the appearance of northern lights, signalling a change in weather.

Northern lights are a northern hemisphere phenomenon of moving lights of various colours in the sky at night. They appear to the Metis viewer as colour-shaded dancing ghosts. When they shift to display a more prominent colour, it means a coming change in the weather. For example, colder weather is signalled by the northern lights' dancing in a prominently red colour, warmer weather by a prominently white colour, and wet weather by a prominent green colour. The coloured weather signals of the northern lights must be combined with other en-vironmenttal weather signs before an accurate weather forecast can be made and used to plan strategies for future activities.

Weather signs such as playful horses and a coloured ring of clouds around the sun, or sun dogs on the sides of the sun, signal rain or snow in two days. The thickness of fur and hair on animals (indicating an insulation value) and the size of a beaver house or a muskrat pushup (indicating an amount of food the animals have stored), are understood as signals for whether a winter will be warm or cold. A beaver house built on high ground signals a wet spring, while one built on low ground signals a dry spring. The harvesting activity of making slough hay was usually completed around the time that berries began to ripen: in the fourth week of July and the first week of August.

Ohpahoo Pesim or Flying Moon

Ohpahoo Pesim or "flying moon" is the month of August. It is the time of year when the young waterfowl and summer birds are old enough to begin to fly, and it signals to my mother that berry-gathering season has arrived. Native berry plants and other local plants and animals follow a seven-year, or lynx, life cycle. In the first year of their life cycle, they are few in number. Each succeeding year they become more numerous, until they reach a maximum population and peak in the seventh year. During the seventh year, the plants and animals usually develop a terminal disease, or will not be fertilized and become barren, or some other phenomenon will prevent a continuous growth pattern. The weak will then perish and only the fittest will survive. Their intangible aspects will return to the spirit world and their tangible aspects will return to the elements of Mother Earth. Through observation and keeping a record of these life cycles, my mother and my father could predict what plants and animals would be in sufficient numbers to be gathered and harvested for the season. Thus, our harvesting did not pose a threat to the species or otherwise cause an imbalance in their life cycle. This year was the season for saskatoon and high-bush cranberry to be gathered.

Gathering enough saskatoon berries for my mother to preserve and can required us to travel by horse team to their various niches in the ecosystem, along the banks of the Boyer River. It was my task to catch and harness the horses, hitch them to the wagon, and drive my mother to the gathering sites. Barney and May, our everyday work team of horses, were full brother and sister to each other. Barney was a bay gelding, very well trained and gentle to handle. May was a white mare, also very well trained, but shy and temperamental to handle. As a result, they made a good matched team.

The first time that my brother and I harnessed them, we had to stand on an overturned five-gallon metal pail in order to reach their necks to buckle the collars and throw on their harness. My younger brother would stand on the other side of the horse from me, and as I lifted the harness onto its back, he would catch a hame strap and pull the harness the rest of the way over. We would then bridle the horses in the same manner, once again standing on the five-gallon metal pail. There were a total of fourteen connections to be made, of buckles, snaps, and chain links, to harness the team to the neck yoke, pole, and eveners that hitched them to pull the wagon. My father taught us to double-check each and every connection and to make sure the driving lines and pulling tugs were not twisted.

Our farm horse wagon was made by Massey Harris. It was a good-quality, everyday-use model. Its wooden spoke wheels were forty-four inches in diameter and its body was twenty-two inches off the ground. The wagon box was made of one by four inch planed shiplap lumber. It had sides three feet high, and was four by twelve feet in size. It had a wooden seat for the teamster. Passengers either sat on the floor or stood. My mother usually sat on the grub box (containing our food and water) on the way to her favourite saskatoon gathering sites.

This saskatoon gathering site was on a forty-acre farm field owned by my father located six miles south of our farmhouse along the Mackenzie Highway. The southern boundary of the land was marked by a creek, the Boyer River, and along its banks grew saskatoon plants. My father had observed these plants to be in full blossom while he was spring planting a wheat crop in the field. He informed my mother of the possible saskatoon crop. She had sent me earlier in the summer to observe whether or not they bore any berries. I remember finding the plants to be loaded with large, juicy, sweet-tasting saskatoons. I had gathered a few for my mother to sample.

We arrived at the site within an hour of leaving home. Before we gathered any saskatoons, my mother said a prayer and offered a pinch of tobacco. My mother was an expert at gathering saskatoon berries. It was impossible for me to keep up with her. She would tie the handle of a tin lard pail around her waist with a white cotton cloth and gather berries using both her hands simultaneously, while walking from tree to tree. Her berry pail was free of leaves and insects, whereas my berry pail never was. Upon filling her pail she would empty its contents into a five-gallon pail, and continue gathering until she determined that it was time for lunch. While we ate our lunch, she would tell stories of earlier experiences gathering. We would have a short nap and continue gathering until she decided it was time to go home for the day.

Upon reaching home, my mother would cook supper for the family and begin cleaning and canning the saskatoon berries. After the supper dishes were cleared off the dining table, she would spread out the berries on a clean tablecloth and begin removing the leaves and insects. The cleaned berries were then washed in a tub of cold water, and put into a gallon pot of sugared water to be cooked at a slow boil on the wood stove. My mother would constantly taste the cooking berries and add more sugar or water until they were cooked to her satisfaction. The cooked berries were then poured into one-quart glass jars and left to cool on the kitchen counter for the night. Once cool, they would be stored in the dirt cellar. She canned sixty quarts of saskatoon berries in this manner before she began to start gathering high-bush cranberries.

The high-bush cranberry gathering site was located within walking distance of our house, so gathering them did not require the use of horses. The berries grew in a boreal forest mixture of spruce, white poplar, and willow trees in an area one mile southwest of our house. Cranberry bushes are two to four feet in height. Their berries are brilliant red in colour and have a bitter taste. My mother's method of gathering them was similar to that for gathering saskatoons, only she had to bend down in order to reach them. This was hard on her back, and so gathering them was a much slower process. The amount harvested was small when compared to the amount of saskatoons. My mother cooked them in the same manner but used more sugar to sweeten their taste. She made pancake syrup from them by straining the berries through a cotton cloth to screen out the pits. The syrup was canned in one-quart glass jars and stored in the dirt cellar.

My mother and father also gathered medicinal plants to be used for health and healing when the time was right to gather them. My family made use of several medicinal plants. Some were gathered in the spring when the sap began to run, or when they were in bloom. Others, such as the bark from the balsam tree, were gathered throughout the year, whenever they were needed. Balsam bark was used to cure a patient suffering from respiratory diseases such as asthma or bronchitis. A piece of balsam bark the size of the patient's hand, and four-inch long roots from a saskatoon plant and a willow tree were boiled into a tea. The patient drank a cup of it every day until the disease was cured. The patient was also required to say a prayer asking Mother Earth and the plant's spirits for their gifts of medicine and thanking them for restoring his or her health. This ceremony and ritual were necessary for all traditional cures. Otherwise the medicine would not be effective.

The rat root plant (*wehkes*) grows in sloughs. It is difficult to find if one is inexperienced and may hide if the proper ritual is not conducted. It is gathered in the fall and used to cure a sore throat. At the first sign of a sore throat, the patient is given a small piece of rat root to chew on. The chewing releases curative juices. During the common cold season, most elderly Metis would carry a piece of rat root with them at all times.

Black poplar buds that sprout in the spring and fall were gathered to treat a patient with a bad burn infection. One year a nephew who came to stay with us accidentally spilt a bowl of hot porridge on his chest, giving himself a bad burn. His skin immediately formed a third-degree burn blister, and within the day he developed a fever. My father immediately began to administer a healing process: he prayed and made a tea by boiling a plant called muskeg tea. This served to lower my nephew's body temperature and to assist his immune system in fighting the developing infection. My father then made a poultice of black poplar buds and applied it to the burnt skin blister. My nephew dropped into a deep sleep. Our family recited the rosary and my mother offered some diamond willow fungus.

My nephew awoke the next morning with a slight fever. I noticed, when my father changed the poultice, that the blister had broken during the night and drained into the poultice. The wound was a bright pink colour. My father informed me that my nephew was responding to the treatment of the muskeg tea and black poplar buds because our prayers had been heard by the plant's spirits, The Great Spirit and his spirit helpers. My father discontinued administering the muskeg tea when my nephew's temperature was back to normal. He continued with the poultice treatment until my nephew's skin was healed. The skin developed a scar tissue during its healing process because it was a third degree burn.

The sap from the white poplar tree was eaten by our family in the springtime when it was running. A family member would choose a white poplar tree about one foot in diameter from the groves that grew on the banks along the creek and with a sharp knife would skin off a portion of its bark. This left an exposed area on the wood from which sap would run. The blade of the knife was used to gather the sap, by running it against the wood, upwards. Sap would accumulate on the knife blade, and then be transferred onto the skinned bark. The person performing the sapping process would usually eat it.

The white poplar tree sap would give the person who digested it a mild form of diarrhoea and in the process cleanse the person's body of unnecessary toxins. The sapping process would be discontinued when the sap stopped running or when the person felt his or her body was thoroughly cleaned of its build-up of toxins from eating winter foods and drinking stagnated water.

Another healing practice of my father's involved using muskrat fur as a treatment for arthritis. My father would harvest a large muskrat in the fall, when its fur was prime. He cured its hide by stretching it over a drying frame. The frame was carved from a piece of board and shaped to fit the body of the muskrat. Its skin was then turned inside out and fitted onto the frame. The fur rested on the board and the skin was exposed to the air to be dried. When the muskrat skin was dried and cured, my father would wrap it around his left shoulder joint, which was often inflamed with arthritis, letting the fur rest on the skin of his joint. The static electricity charge and the natural qualities of the muskrat fur would treat his arthritis. My father administered this traditional treatment and recited a daily prayer until his shoulder joint was healed.

My mother administered home remedies to us children whenever we came down with an illness, although for serious illnesses we were treated by the local health nurse or taken to Dr. Mary Jackson who had a medical practice at Keg River. I do not recall being seriously sick as a child. The worst illnesses that I can recall were common colds that developed into chest colds. My mother would make me drink an herbal tea made of wild mint and honey, rub my chest with Vick's VapoRub and apply a hot-water bottle wrapped in a flannel cloth to my chest. She would make a bed on the chesterfield in the living room, cover me with a comforter, and keep me home from school for the day. By mid-afternoon, this treatment would loosen the congestion in my chest. I would be up and around and well enough to do my daily chores.

Nochetowi Pesim or Mating Moon

The gathering season for berries passed as the month of August came to an end, bringing in *nochetowi pesim*, "mating moon," or the month of September. September was one of the busiest times of the year for the Metis. It was the time when the gifted harvesters of the community worked from dawn to dusk, Monday to Saturday, harvesting garden vegetables, cereal grain crops, and domestic and wild animals. Sunday was a day of rest, visiting, and going to church. The garden vegetables were harvested by our family. We worked collectively to dig the tuberous plants. Every day after coming home from school we would have lunch, change from our school clothes into our work clothes, and receive instructions from my mother or my father for chores to perform.

One of my chores was to clean out the vegetable bins located in the dirt storage cellar of our house. The trap door for the cellar was in front of the cupboards in the kitchen. It was made of a double layer of boards covered with linoleum floor covering. It had a brass lifting ring recessed into its surface and was double-hinged to the floor. It was a heavy structure to open, and once opened it was held up with a wooden prop. The stairs leading down to the cellar, as well as the vegetable bins and canning storage shelves, were all constructed of rough-sawed two by ten spruce boards. The floor had no covering. The trap-door frame was large enough to allow light into the cellar, so a lantern was not necessary. I would fill an old galvanized tub with soil, roots, and decaying vegetables from the bins and haul the contents to be dumped into the potato garden plot. After this chore was completed, I would nail the vegetable chute into place and wait for the vegetables to be poured down the chute and tumble into their respective bins. I would hand-place them, to ensure that the bins were evenly filled. Sometimes I would assist with digging the crop of turnips, carrots, beets, and potatoes.

These vegetables were manually dug with a six-tine pitchfork. The method was to align the fork near the vegetable and press it downward with your body weight by applying your foot on its frame. You then lifted the fork with the vegetables and soil and turned it over, emptying them onto the ground. The vegetables were shaken or rubbed free of soil and their leafy tops cut off. In a dry fall, the vegetables were put into a galvanized tub, loaded onto a stoneboat, hauled by a horse to the house, unloaded, and emptied down the chute into their storage bin. In a wet fall, the dug vegetables were left to dry in the sun and then stored. My mother and father harvested smaller vegetables, such as peas, beans, onions and corn, during the day when I was in school. My mother would preserve these vegetables by canning or storing them in their shells in the cellar.

After the vegetables were harvested, my father would begin to harvest the cereal grains with a farm machine called a binder. The binder was a complicated machine, operated by my father. An older sister would drive the small farm tractor used to pull it. The binder had many turning pulleys, link chains, a canvas conveyer belt on a four by eight foot turntable, a turning reel made of wooden slats, and a cutting knife. This machine cut the grain stocks three feet in length and six inches above the ground. The turning reel laid the stocks onto the canvas conveyer belt, which carried them up to a section that tied the stocks into grain bundles eighteen inches in diameter. The bundles were deposited, one at a time, onto a carrier. The carrier was tripped by a foot pedal when six bundles accumulated on it and these were deposited on the ground into rows, and stooked, or stood upright to dry.

My brother-in-law, the husband of my oldest sister, was employed by my father to gather the pile of six grain bundles into stooks. Stooking was performed by grasping a bundle under each arm and standing them up so they came to rest on each other with the grain heads upward and their bases forming a triangle on the stubble field. A well-made stook could withstand any wind, repel rainwater, and complete the ripening of the grain. As a green wheat bundle could weigh as much as fifty pounds, my brother-in-law had to be in excellent physical condition to stook ten to fifteen acres of wheat bundles in a day. Barley and oats bundles are lighter and do not require as much physical energy to stook them. After all the crops were cut, stooked, and ripened by the sun and wind, it was time for threshing the grain.

Threshing grain was the process of separating kernels from husks and stocks by passing it through a threshing machine. This machine, operated by an older brother, resembled a large tin box. It had an opening at the front end and a large and a small spout on the back end, and was powered by a forty-foot belt driven by the flywheel belt pulley of a tractor. The grain bundles were pitch forked into the front end, fed onto a chain-link conveyer belt, carried through four large, double-bladed knives churning on an offset shaft, and cut into various sections. The smaller pieces of straw, chaff, and grain kernels then rolled and tumbled through a series of moving smaller knives and screens with air generated by a large metal fan. This process separated the grain kernels from the other debris. The grain was poured through the smaller spout into the grain bin. The straw and chaff were blown through the larger spout into a straw pile. The threshing machine was very loud and generated a cloud of grain dust. Its moving parts had to be continually greased and checked for breaks, its screen widths reset, and its blades resharpened and cleaned.

My after-school chore during this season was to assist my older brother with operating the threshing machine. I would clean the build-up of straw and chaff from under the threshing machine. I had to be careful not to get tangled up in its moving parts. The build-up of grain underneath the auger spout in the grain bin had to be shovelled to other sections of the bin. It was constant work to shovel it when the bin was nearly full. The angle of the spout blowing straw into a pile had to be raised as the straw pile grew in size, otherwise the straw would plug the threshing machine.

Other times I was assigned to work as a field pitcher. The field pitcher's duty was to assist the teamsters with loading grain bundles from the stooks in the fields onto their hayracks pulled by a team of horses. The team of horses was trained to walk undriven alongside the row of stooks, stop at the command of "whoa," and wait until the teamster and the field pitcher pitchforked the grain bundles onto the hayrack before moving on. We arranged the bundles to allow the maximum number to be loaded onto the hayrack, then drove to the threshing machine and fed the bundles into it. That year we had four teams hauling the grain bundles.

My mother's responsibility was to cook the three big meals and two lunches a day to feed the threshing crew. She rose at 5:00 a.m. to cook a full-course breakfast, made a lunch of sandwiches and coffee at 10:00 a.m., a full-course dinner at noon, another lunch of sandwiches and coffee at 3:00 p.m., and a full-course supper at 7:00 p.m. She would bring lunch and coffee out to the threshing machine. When the teamsters finished unloading, they would stop for a half-hour lunch break. Her sandwiches tasted better than any others that I have had since.

After the threshing season was over, it was time to harvest a steer and a hog for our winter's supply of meat. This year we decided to butcher a two-year-old Hereford steer that my father had raised on the farm from a calf. After the steer was harvested, it was raised by the hind legs with a block and tackle, connected to a tripod constructed of wooden poles, and hung a foot off the ground. The hanging carcass was skinned starting at the hind legs so that the hide fell off in folds towards the neck. The intestines were carefully removed by making an incision at the base of the groin and cutting downward to the rib cage. They would then fall into a galvanized tub. The heart, liver, kidneys, and the big stomach were considered to be the most precious gifts of the animal and were retrieved to be eaten. The carcass was left to hang until it had sufficiently cooled and was then cut into various cuts of meat, such as stew, steaks, roasts, and ribs. Using a hand-cranked meat grinder, my mother made hamburger from the pieces of meat which did not make the various other cuts. The prepared meat was wrapped and stored in the meat house.

Then a hog was harvested. The carcass of the hog was dipped into a forty-five-gallon barrel of hot water to soften its skin, so that its hair could be removed by scraping with a knife blade. You grasped the knife blade between both hands, applying slight pressure and pulling it towards you. On areas of the carcass where the hair was difficult to remove, a gunny sack soaked in hot water was applied to soften the skin so that the hair could be removed. The meat was prepared in the same manner as the beef and stored in the meat house for the winter.

September was also the month that the moose began their annual rut. A Metis moose harvester from within the community would be one of the first men to find a moose rutting sign; a stand of willow trees with skinned bark indicating that a moose was there to scrape off dried skin from its antlers, or a rut wallow, or the sound of a bull moose mating call. He would then inform others that the moose had begun to "run." These signs signalled that it was time to go on an annual fall moose harvest. A group of four Metis men, including one of my older brothers, would leave in horse and wagon to set up a harvesting camp somewhere in the boreal forest surrounding the community. The first day of harvest they would set out from camp, some on foot and some on horseback, to sight moose. They would determine their sex and age range, and decide which moose were to be harvested the next day. The next morning before sunrise, the harvesters performed a final harvesting prayer and food offering before leaving camp. This would ensure a successful moose harvest. The group would remain at the camp until all were successful in a moose harvest and the meat was properly prepared. They then returned to the community.

Upon returning, the harvesters would distribute and share a large portion of the moose meat with other Metis, beginning with the elders, the next of kin, the most in need, and finally others that had shared with them in the past. My father informed me that when the community was first established in 1939, a gifted harvester spent most of the year harvesting moose to keep the incoming families supplied with fresh meat.

A gifted moose harvester did not keep the entire moose meat for his own family. To do so would abuse his gift, and so he might not be as successful in the future.

September was also the month waterfowl began to flock and feed in the farm fields preparing to make their fall migration back to the south. The community of Paddle Prairie was founded on an old dried lake bottom which had evolved over time, creating a prairie with fertile, rock-free black topsoil to an average depth of twelve inches, and a habitat for many species of plants and animals. The migrating waterfowl and summer birds used the original lake as a stop-over, to rest and feed in the spring and fall. These birds now use the prairie. Ducks and geese are the main waterfowl that are fall harvested. Other birds, such as grouse and prairie chicken, were traditionally harvested throughout the year. Prairie chickens were once abundant, but now only a few remain, and so they are no longer harvested. The Metis believe that their population was destroyed by DDT.

Kuskutino Pesim or Freezing Moon

With the busy month of September coming to an end, there is a noticeable change in the weather which brings in kuskutino pesim, "freezing moon," and the month of October. This month was the time to repair buildings and equipment for the coming winter. All of our barns used for sheltering the farm animals were constructed with saddle-notched dried spruce logs, fitted one on top of the other, which created an uneven wall thickness. The roofs of the barns were constructed of spruce slabs except for the chicken coop, which had a sod roof. The space between the saddle-notched wall logs was filled in with a mixture of water, clay, long-stemmed grass, and horse manure. As this mixture dried, it shrank and would fall out. This insulation had to be replaced in October through a process called "mudding."

My father had found a source of clay on our farm which had the binding quality required to hold the mixture together. My father measured correct proportions of this clay, grass, horse manure, and water and mixed them in a galvanized tub. The mixture was scooped into pails and hauled to the barns, where we applied it with gloved hands into the spaces between the logs. After a week of hard work, the barns were all mudded and repaired for the cold winter weather.

When the ground was sufficiently frozen by the nightly frosts of October to allow for a loaded horse wagon to travel without becoming stuck in a mud hole, slough hay and firewood were freighted home. My older brothers freighted the slough hay back to the farm on two farm wagons outfitted with hayracks. They would leave the farm at 8:00 a.m. for the hay meadow and pitchfork a haystack onto each of the hayracks before lunch. They would return to the farm and unload the hay into the hay loft of the barn or the hay corral before retiring for the day at 8:00 p.m. When all the hay was hauled back to the farm they would begin hauling firewood.

Hauling firewood was a much more labour-intensive activity than hauling hay. Two farm wagons were outfitted with wooden bunks large enough to haul two cords of wood, measuring two by four by sixteen feet. The reaches extended four feet, to allow for dry white poplar trees to be hauled. My older brothers would leave for the site where the dry white poplar trees would be felled and loaded onto the wagons around 7:00 a.m. The method of felling the dry trees would be either by axe, by Swede saw, or by crosscut saw. When enough trees had been felled, they were skidded by a single horse back to a landing site, cut into lengths, and lifted onto the wagons. When the loads became too high, the trees had to be rolled up two slanting poles with a cant hook. It required a long day of hard work to gather four cords of dry firewood in this manner.

My brothers returned to the farm after daylight. After darkness fell, my father would send me outside the house to listen for the noise of the wagon wheels rolling on frozen ground and attempt to determine whether my brothers were on their way home. The dry trees were unloaded onto a woodpile near our house.

When my father decided that the supply of firewood gathered was sufficient to last us for the year, we buzz-sawed it into lengths that would fit the cookstove and heater. My father would hire the community-owned John Deere tractor and buzz saw to cut the firewood. My older brothers would lift a sixteen-foot dry tree onto the table of the buzz saw. The operator standing on the other side of the rotating saw blade would cut the tree into pieces of the required length and throw them onto a pile. It took one day for the crew to cut all the corded wood. After school was out for the day, my younger brother and I would stack the wood into rows.

Our daily chores involved chopping and hauling wood to fill the woodboxes located behind the cookstove and heater. I would chop the wood into various pieces sized to fit into the fireboxes of the stoves, and my younger brother would haul them, stacked in the cradle of his arm, into the house.

Yekopew Pesim or Hoarfrost Moon

Hauling slough hay and firewood would be completed in the first week of *yekopew pesim*, "hoarfrost moon," and the month of November. My older brothers would leave to work outside the community in a sawmill for the winter months. My father, my younger brothers, and I would be left with the responsibility to feed and water the livestock. My mother would begin her Christmas baking in the second week of November. She acquired her knowledge of baking while in Mission School at Grouard, Alberta, and from her aunt.

My mother would bake cookies, pies, and a Christmas cake. Her cookies were ginger snaps, her pies were mincemeat and raisin, and her Christmas cake was made from a home recipe of dried fruits, nuts, spices, sugar, water, brandy or rum, baking powder, and flour. She would measure these ingredients with a glass measuring cup, mix them in a large metal baking bowl into a stiff cake dough, and proportion the mixture into six square metal cake pans of different sizes. The cake would be baked at a steady temperature in the oven of the wood cookstove, and while it was baking, my mother would not allow us to run or jump in the house for fear that the movement would cause the cake to fall. She would test the baking cake, by piercing its middle with a toothpick to determine whether it was thoroughly cooked. If the withdrawn toothpick contained any dough on its surface, then the cake was not baked enough; if it came out dry, the cake was cooked.

When the Christmas fruitcake was cooked, my mother laid it on brown paper and left it to cool on the kitchen table. Once the cake was cool, she wrapped it in the brown paper, along with the cookies and pies. She also threw in an apple to keep them moist. She stored them in a ten-gallon metal cream container in the dirt cellar to age until Christmas Day. On Christmas Eve, the baking was retrieved from storage and served for dessert. The Christmas fruitcake was served in a hot sauce and eaten after our turkey dinner.

My father bought large quantities of food supplies that could not be gathered or harvested off the land outside the community, with money obtained from selling our farm produce. My father's cash crops, wheat, cattle, and hogs, were shipped to a market at Grimshaw, Alberta. There my father purchased flour and sugar in 100-pound sacks for our family. Eight hundred pounds of flour and two hundred pounds of sugar would be required to feed us for one year. He would also purchase cases of apples, peaches, and plums, which my mother would preserve through canning. Smaller quantities of processed food and some of our clothing were purchased at the community-owned general store.

Clothing that the store did not keep in stock was mail-ordered through a Simpson-Sears, Eaton's, or Army and Navy catalogue. A freight truck, owned and operated by non-Metis living in Peace River, delivered store supplies and mail weekly to the general store and post office in the community. My mother ordered our Christmas gifts in December from the Christmas edition of the catalogues and stored them in her bedroom until Christmas Eve.

Pawastun Pesim or Snow-Drifting Moon

Pawastun pesim, "snow-drifting moon" and the month of December is when the cold weather arrives from the north. The temperature can get down to -40°F by the middle of the month. At this time of the year, I remember settling into a daily routine of attending school and doing my chores. I would rise every weekday morning at 7:00 a.m., get dressed, go downstairs, light the coal-oil lamp, and put more wood into the heater to stoke up the fire that my father had kept fuelled throughout the night. I could tell if the fire had burned out, because a thin sheet of ice would have formed on the water pail sitting on the wash table. I would make a fire in the cookstove with kindling that my younger brother had prepared, and put the water kettle on it to boil. My younger brother would soon rise and begin to make porridge, while I went out to the barn with my dog, Rex. I carried a coal-oil lantern for light as I fed the livestock in the morning darkness.

I would first feed the milk cow and other young cattle tied in stalls in the barn. I would then fork hay from the haystacks into a feeding area for the cattle and horses that wintered outside. Then I would milk the cow. I would untie her calf from its stall, and let it suckle on one side of her udder while I milked the other side into a galvanized milk pail. She gave us about two quarts of milk every morning and every evening, which was used for our cream, butter and milk. When I returned to the house my mother would also be up, having made breakfast of pancakes, bacon, eggs, and birch tree sap syrup or saskatoons. This food would be waiting for me on the table.

I would carefully wash my hands and face before sitting down to eat. After breakfast I would leave for school with my two younger brothers. Against my mother's advice, we usually ran the three-quarters of a mile to school, which gave us a short while to play before classes started. At the lunch break, we would run back to our house for a hot meal before running back to school. We returned home again at about 3:30 p.m., to have a light meal and begin our evening chores. My evening chores were to split the firewood, clean out the barn of manure, add a new bedding of straw, put the barn animals back in their stalls, feed the livestock, and milk the cow again. My father fed and took care of the hogs and chickens, released the barn animals for the day, watered the livestock, and did a variety of other activities when we were in school. After our chores were completed for the day, we began our school homework sitting at a round oak dining table in the living room. We would have supper, finish our homework, and say our family prayers before going to bed at 8:00 p.m. As Christmas Day and our Christmas school holidays approached, I would begin to feel the excitement and spirit of the ceremony and ritual that they brought.

Two Saturdays before Christmas Day, my younger brother and I performed the ritual of selecting a spruce tree, from among the thousand that grew a mile from our house, that would become our Christmas tree. We left the house after daylight. We walked in a single line through snow up to our knees across a farm field and entered the forest. I broke the trail and carried the axe.

In 1960 the weather was bitterly cold. I remember a sharp wind blowing from the northwest into our faces, which made it seem colder than the -30°F on our thermometer. We walked down the centre of an old, abandoned road trying to find the perfect Christmas tree. The trees were all covered with snow, which made them look as though their branches were all evenly spaced and symmetrical,. But when we shook the snow off, the branches revealed themselves to be different and uneven. We spread out, and walked amongst the trees. When we thought that we had found a good tree, we hollered to the others to come and see, only to decide that it was not the one to be selected.

If our winter boots were not properly laced and secured around our ankles, then snow would enter from their tops, melt from our body heat, and wet our wool socks. I remember that my youngest brother's feet began to get cold, and we had to start back to the house before they became frozen. It always seemed to turn out that the first spruce tree we looked at would be the one to be selected, and this year was no different.

On the way home I half carried and half dragged the frozen six-foot tree, trying to not break off too many branches in the process. My mother, anticipating that we would be cold and hungry, fired up the heater and gave us a cup of hot chocolate milk and some cookies. She brought out the cardboard box containing Christmas decorations, and we began to decorate the house and tree. My father started to practice singing the Christmas carols which were sung at midnight mass on Christmas Eve, as he led the community's Roman Catholic church choir.

My father and mother were spiritual people who practiced a syncretic form of religion. They combined the local traditional spiritual beliefs with Christian spiritual beliefs on holy days and at mass. The birth of Christ was a religious celebration in our house. Prayers and hymns were said and sung in both Cree and English. My parent's spiritual influence led me to act as an altar boy for five years. I considered it an honour to be chosen by the priest to carry baby Jesus to the altar and serve at Christmas midnight mass. The team of horses pulled our bobsleigh to church. We usually arrived an hour early to assist the priest with the final preparations. The church was packed with Metis from the community. There was standing room only for latecomers.

After midnight mass was over, my mother's custom was to invite the priest over to our house for a full-course turkey dinner with all the trimmings. My mother made her turkey stuffing from scratch and no other food compares to the taste of her cooking. At this meal she would allow us to open one Christmas gift: an item of clothing. In the morning, the only other gift we opened was a toy. Our Christmas stockings would be stuffed with an apple, an orange, various hard nuts and peanuts, and striped white, red, and green curled Christmas candy. People from the community would drop in throughout Christmas Day to express their wishes to my parents. We children were allowed to visit some friends and compare gifts.

Kese Pesim or Cold Moon

New Year's Eve ended December and brought in *kese pesim*, "cold moon" and the month of January. The ceremony and ritual of a midnight mass performed on New Year's Eve ushered in the new year, and the community celebrated the holiday by holding a dance. We would attend the dance with my mother, and greet people with "Happy New Year." We expressed our spiritual feelings with the custom of kissing the females and shaking hands with the males. After the festivities of Christmas, New Year's and the school holidays were over, it was back to school and my daily chores.

Mikisiw Pesim or Eagle Moon

The months of January and *mikisiw pesim*, "eagle moon," the month of February, were the longest months of the year for me. The cold weather and short daylight hours kept me inside the house most of the time. The days seemed to drag. In the fourth week of February, someone in the community would spot a bald eagle-the first sign that winter was coming to an end.

COMMENTARY

FROM my narrative reflection of these 1960 events, several patterns emerge. There is a seasonal round of activities involving making a living with the land. Through these activities it is clear that the essence of my relationships with my family was primarily spiritual. They were based upon the local traditions of preparing and sharing gifts obtained from the land. The Great Spirit was the donor of these gifts of food, which consisted of the aspects of the mind, emotion, spirit, and body of plants and animals. My family were the recipients. This concept of Spirit Gifting was incorporated into every activity of livelihood, through ceremony, ritual, and sacrifice, which made it possible for my family to live a happy and healthy life throughout this year. I was taught to respect the land, plants, and animals because we were created with all the same aspects, adapted to live in the same environment, and were equal as gifts to one another.

I was educated inside the community from grades one to nine, and my peer group and classmates were all Metis. During this period my Metis traditional worldview had not changed. I began to experience a shift in worldview when I left the community in 1962 to continue my education and to begin employment. This was the first time in my life that I experienced living as a minority, first in the classroom and later in the workplace.

The language spoken in both these places was English, and my education was primarily based upon concepts from Western knowledge. As a result I began to repress my Cree language and traditional knowledge (*emic*) and to adopt a different cultural perspective on life, that of Western knowledge (*etic*). In short, my worldview was changing on a subconscious level. By the time I returned to my community in 1974, I had repressed my sacred worldview, of making a living *with* the land, and had replaced it with a secular worldview, of making a living *off* the land. The following narrative will describe this pattern of making a living.

CHAPTER THREE: LIVING OFF THE LAND

THE SEASON OF NATURAL GAS FIELD CONSTRUCTION

IN 1976, the community of Paddle Prairie had an early snowfall. September brought the snow and it stayed for the winter. In previous years the snow had thawed, and the freezing cycle of October had frozen the land, allowing the heavy equipment used in the construction of natural gas fields to pass without becoming mired in mud and muskeg. The early snowfall acted as insulation, and prevented the land from freezing.

However, oil companies with winter drilling programs on the Settlement insisted upon beginning their winter work early, before the proper freeze-up. This led to my being out in my three-quarter-ton truck conducting field work on dangerously unfrozen ground. I needed to prepare a construction bid on work the oil companies had posted in the Settlement office.

From 1968 to 1974, I had worked for several employers as a civil engineering technologist: the federal government, a municipal government, and a civil engineering consulting firm. I designed and supervised the construction of infrastructures such as roads, bridges, and water and sanitary sewer mains. I now relied upon this civil engineering work experience to assist me in estimating and drafting construction bids.

Making the Bid

I was taking the chance of getting the truck stuck on the unfrozen bush road, but I decided to take the risk, as I needed the money. Oilfield work had become my livelihood. I left my father's residence at 6:00 a.m. in the morning and drove as near as possible to the proposed natural gas well location. From there I proceeded on foot to assess what heavy construction equipment would be required to do the work. On my way home after completing the assessment, the back end of my truck became stuck in a low spot on the bush road, about fifteen miles from the nearest residence. There was no hope of getting a tow out of the mud hole. The only alternative was to jack up the rear wheels of the truck and fill in the ruts made by the tires with short lengths of wood cut from dead trees. It took three hours of labouring with my power saw to cut enough wood to build up the ruts. I was finally able to drive over the mud hole, and continue on home to work on the bid.

Using a forestry map of the proposed natural gas wellsite location, empirical data from my field notes, and Polaroid pictures taken of the natural resources, topography, and forestry, I began to carefully analyze the information. I had to determine the technology, or necessary equipment, and labour which were required to complete the work and prepare a cost estimate. The job was to construct, by clear-cutting, piling, and burning vegetation, one-quarter mile of winter road, a three-acre wellsite area, and a half-acre campsite area, as well as to dig a sump pit. Unlike the use of spring fires for cleansing the land, the use of heavy equipment would scar the land. These areas had been previously surveyed by the oil company. The boundaries were marked and outlined with red fluorescent survey flagging.

Fortunately, the topography of the land was level to gently undulating. However, it also contained a section of muskeg that the road had to span in order to reach the location proposed for a wellsite. The forestry was medium-density white spruce, white poplar, willow, and black spruce. The land showed signs of supporting wildlife such as moose, rabbit, coyote, and squirrel. Winter birds of the area included the whiskey jack, chickadee, and raven, some of whose habitats would be destroyed by clear-cutting the forest.

There was also a skidoo track meandering throughout the region, indicating that a local trapper was harvesting the area for mink and martin fur. The clear-cut would also interfere with his trap line, as the noise made by the heavy machines would drive away these fur-bearing animals. The trapper would not receive any compensation for this loss of income. Although the work would have all of these effects, all of its activities were conducted according to Alberta forestry and environmental regulations for oilfield construction and the Settlement's surface rights policy.

The winter road was to be constructed to a sixty-foot right-of-way. This meant that it would consist of an open pathway through the bush sixty feet wide, with the brush clear-cut and windrowed to one side of the road. There would be a firebreak every 500 feet, the width of a crawler tractor dozer blade. The firebreak in the brush pile would provide access to wildlife for crossing the clear-cut roadway. The bush line was to be cleaned of overhanging trees. The bush on the wellsite and campsite locations was also to be clear-cut, pushed into a pile, and burned. The sump pit was to be dug six feet deep and thirty feet square. I estimated that the heavy equipment required to do the work would be two caterpillar crawler tractors, or "Cats," of different sizes and with different attachments.

I already owned some heavy construction equipment, such as a D6C Cat. This Cat was equipped with power shift, wide pad, a dozer blade, and a winch. D6C refers to the Cat's size and model, and power shift means that it shifted gears automatically. Wide pad means that it has a thirty-three-inch track width. A dozer blade is an attachment used to push and cut materials, and a winch is an attachment used to pull the Cat or other equipment if they become stuck or are unable to move under their own power. The wide pads enable the Cat to travel on soft, unfrozen ground.

My strategy for using this equipment was to bulldoze a trail into the site which would remove the snow and expose the ground. This exposure would allow the ground to freeze sufficiently so that it could support a D7A Cat, a piece of equipment that has more horsepower than a D6C. I needed one equipped with a dozer blade and a ripper. A ripper is an attachment used to rip frozen ground so that it can be moved, or to rip out large tree stumps. The D7A Cat was to be used for clear-cutting the larger trees and to dig the sump pit. This equipment would have to be hired or rented. The other equipment required for the job would be two power saws and a truck to haul fuel and tools. The labour power or men required would be four heavy-equipment operators, as I planned to operate a double shift, and two power-saw men. They would all be hired from the community's labour supply. I would act as the construction foreman to this six-man crew.

A double shift refers to working the Cats two ten-hour periods or shifts in one day. The day shift began at 7:00 a.m. and ended at 6:00 p.m., with the operators, or "Cat skinners," taking one hour off at noon to eat their lunch. The evening shift began at 7:00 p.m. and ended at 6:00 a.m., the Cat skinners taking one hour off at midnight for their lunch. The Cat skinners were responsible for operating and cleaning their Cats according to the equipment specifications. As the contractor, I was responsible for equipment maintenance and repair. Experienced Cat skinners can accomplish a large amount of work in one day, if they know how to work at the machine's speed and take pride in their operating abilities. Skinners can make or break a contractor. This means they can make you money or lose you money. If the proper social relationships are established between the contractor and his or her Cat skinners, the company will be successful.

The Cat skinners that I would ask to work for me on this contract were all men from the community whom I had known since childhood. They were all about ten years older than I was, and had been operating heavy equipment for the past ten to fifteen years in oilfield work off the Settlement. Thus they had considerably more experience in this type of work than I did. However, I had what they referred to as "engineering knowledge," and so was qualified to plan and coordinate the job.

I planned to offer a higher hourly rate to my skinners to increase their take-home pay. I also decided to give them advances if required between their biweekly pay cheques, and to treat them as fellow Metis. The skinners all had families to support, while I was single and lived with my parents. If one of them required time off for sickness or personal reasons, I would operate his shift myself rather than hire another Cat skinner. The two power-saw men were also from the community. I also offered them the going hourly rate, but would work them only during the day shift because operating a power saw at night is dangerous.

Each of the employees was to supply his own transportation to and from the work site, bring a lunch, and live at home. This avoided the need to supply a work camp. For complying with this system they would receive a set amount of money per day over and above their wages, referred to as a "living allowance."

Having determined the heavy construction equipment and labour required for the contract, my next task was to estimate the time required to complete the job. This involves knowing how much work the machines and men can perform when working at an average output for one hour. The work includes cutting, piling, and burning brush on the work site and excavating the sump pit at the wellsite. The total hours of work are then multiplied by the going oilfield rates in dollars per hour for the two machines, the service truck, the two power saws, and the labour, to derive a gross profit figure. The net profit is determined by subtracting the expenses incurred in performing the work from the gross profit. If the contractor considers the net profit too small to take the risk of doing the work, then he can inflate the gross profit amount. Net profit is the ultimate incentive for the contractor to take the risk of doing oilfield work.

However, the goal of the landman, an employee of the oil company, is to get the work done for the least cost in the shortest time. The landman's primary responsibility is to obtain permission for right-of-entry onto Settlement lands for the oil company. Such permission allows a company to explore for deposits of natural gas, drill gas wells, and construct facilities to produce the natural gas for export to markets off the Settlement. As well, the landman has influence in deciding what contractor is awarded a contract for construction of the infrastructure. For these reasons the landman is recognized as having "power."

Right-of-entry is negotiated under the Settlement's surface rights policy, a set of guidelines used to determine the amount of compensation the Settlement receives from the oil company for use of Settlement lands. The surface rights policy was developed from Regulation 116/60 of the *Metis Betterment Act* (originally the *Metis Population Betterment Act*) entitled "Regulations Governing Trapping and Hunting of Game and Fur-Bearing Animals upon Lands Set Aside for Occupation by a Metis Settlement Association, Section 5." This regulation gives the Settlement Council, the local government body of the Metis Settlement, the legal right to decide who other than Settlement members should enter or sojourn upon any area set aside for Metis Settlement to do business or carry on work of any nature.

Compensation or value for right-of-entry is determined as a yearly monetary amount given for the loss of use of the land by the Settlement during the lifetime of the natural gas field. Also considered when determining compensation are any employment or business opportunities for Settlement members. Work which Settlement members cannot undertake because of a lack of proper technology, such as drilling, testing, and pipe lining, is awarded to outside contractors by the oil company. The goal of the oil company is to get the natural gas field into production on time, at minimum cost and maximum profit.

The oil company begins a natural gas project by bidding on the mineral rights of provincial Crown land put up for sale by the provincial government. In this instance, the lands were those set aside as a Metis Settlement at Paddle Prairie. Ownership of these lands is an unresolved issue between the Metis members of the Settlement and the officials of the provincial government, because they have different opinions of what "ownership" means.

Ownership and the Land

Ownership (*tipeyichiwin*) to the Metis is viewed as a gift of collective stewardship for Mother Earth, a living being, from The Great Spirit (*Kechi Manitow*). This stewardship descended through our ancestors, allowing us to make a happy and healthy livelihood in a relationship with the land. Metis in turn pass the gift of stewardship on to their children and grandchildren for their collective use. No monetary value is attached to this spiritual concept of "ownership." Deceased Metis elder Adrian Hope described his thoughts on this con-cept as follows: "We belong to the land; the land does not belong to us."

The meaning of "ownership" to the government officials, who are responsible for administration of the *Metis Betterment Act* and its regulations, is a different one. For them, ownership is the legal right of dominion, possession, and proprietorship of Settlement land by the Crown.

The legal opinion of the government officials in 1976 was that the Metis Settlements are Crown lands temporarily set aside for the exclusive occupation and use of the Metis population of Alberta. The Metis were granted different forms of surface rights, but the Crown retained mineral rights and underlying title. The Paddle Prairie Metis Settlement Council, along with seven other Metis Settlement Councils, was in the process of forming a federation to oppose collectively this legal opinion of the provincial government. The Federation of Metis Settlements' legal and sacred opinion is that Metis Aboriginal title existed as a gift from The Great Spirit to the Metis prior to the creation of dominion of the province of Alberta and the country of Canada. The Metis Aboriginal title is a spiritual gift, and so cannot be extinguished or sold by living human beings. The future will decide whose concept of ownership is accepted.

The Politics of Financial Success

Once the landman is granted permission for right-of-entry by the Settlement to drill for natural gas, he returns to his head office in Calgary, Alberta. There the final decision is made as to who is awarded a contract for construction work. There were three other Metis contractors bidding for this particular work. In order to be successful in beating the competition, I had to know how an oil company conducted business.

I knew that the lowest bid does not necessarily get the contract, so I began a public relations campaign with the oil company's landman and construction supervisor. I wanted to try to convince them that I could best perform their work. Overnight, the landman and construction supervisor became my "best friends." I treated my fellow Metis contractors whom I had known all of my life, as opponents who had to be outperformed. I made a trip to the oil company's head office, where I wined and dined the oilmen. I used this opportunity to impress upon them my engineering experience, my capability to supervise and complete contracts, and my record of performing satisfactory work. I also had to keep my bank manager informed on possible contracts, as well as the manager of the heavy equipment company, where I had entered into a rental purchase agreement for my D6C Cat. They wanted assurance that there would be a sufficient cash flow to make monthly payments on my line of credit and the payroll.

These businessmen were aware that, as a Metis contractor, I could not use my land allotment, termed "unmovable property," as collateral for credit. I did not have fee simple title under the *Metis Betterment Act*. I could only use "moveable property," such as equipment with clear title and domesticated cattle and grain, if I were fortunate enough to have possession of such collateral. I also would have to lobby the Settlement Council to put in a good word on my behalf to the oilmen.

If I had played my community politics right by supporting the majority of the Council members in their bid to get elected onto the Settlement Council, then I could seek their political support for my bid. If I did not have the support of the majority of these political decision-makers, I would have to rely totally upon my ability to influence the oilmen to decide in my favour.

Although contractors could be Council members, they would then have to exclude themselves from negotiations with the oil company for right-of-entry permission. Otherwise, other contractors could accuse them of conflict of interest, because they could stand to gain monetarily from decisions that might favour the oil company. A successful contractor on the Settlement usually had political, social, and economic influence at all levels where decisions were made. In my experience, the most difficult decision that the Settlement membership and contractors had to make was to give permission for oil companies to enter Settlement lands for the purpose of natural gas field development.

The Settlement's membership and Council were concerned with the socio-economic impacts of natural gas development on their livelihood. The questions on everyone's minds were whether natural gas development would have positive impacts for employment and business opportunities, and whether the positive impacts would offset the negative impacts on Metis livelihood. During this period no questions were asked about how this development would affect the sacred relationship with the land.

In order to deal adequately with the legal issues of the *Metis Betterment Act* and regulations on these matters, the Settlement hired a law firm. We chose one that specialized in surface rights for natural gas development and could negotiate with the oil company's lawyers. For socio-economic questions the Settlement relied upon its membership, and held general meetings for those interested in obtaining or discussing natural gas field work. The central issue of the discussions was how to develop a strategy to convince the oil company that the Settlement's labour force and contractors were capable of performing natural gas field work. The negative impact of this development was viewed as not getting the potential employment and business opportunities created by the work. No one considered the impact upon the land and our relationship to it.

The oil company's landman and construction supervisor were not convinced that Metis had the work ethic to get the job done on time and at cost. In order to get the work for its membership, the Settlement decided to deny permission for right-of-entry to Settlement land to any oil company that would not give employment and business opportunities to those Settlement members who were interested in and capable of doing a portion of the work. The oil company and the current outside contractors the company wanted to bring onto the Settlement were forced to take the chance that the Settlement contractors could clear-cut, pile, and burn bush from right-of-way construction. The Settlement also stipulated that the oil company must post all contract work in the Settlement office, and that only Settlement contractors would be allowed to bid on this work.

The initial doubt that Metis could possess a Western work ethic was quickly dispelled by the Metis contractors. We demonstrated to the oilmen that clear-cutting, piling, and burning brush was not a difficult task if trees, plants, and wildlife habitat were not viewed as a sacred gift, but rather as something that had to be removed with the use of Cats in order for the oil company to develop natural gas for export. The Metis contractors accepted this change from a sacred to a secular worldview of the bush, if they wanted to make a living in this way. When my bid for the work was accepted by the oil company, I also repressed my previous sacred worldview and accepted a secular one.

The Contract

I received notice two months after I submitted my bid that I had been awarded the oilfield work. I immediately implemented my construction plan and critical timeline for completing the job. My construction crew and I were anxious to start making money. I arose every morning at 5:00 a.m., cooked a breakfast, made a thermos of coffee and a lunch to be eaten on the job, and left for the work site at 6:00 a.m. Upon reaching the job site, I fuelled up the Cats from a Tidy Tank of fuel on the back of my pick-up truck. Meanwhile the Cat skinners checked the level of engine oil and the power-shift oil and cleaned the tracks of mud. The machine had its engine shut off for a thirty-minute period and was back working within the hour with a fresh Cat skinner to operate it. Machines do not tire, but people do.

The power-saw men started fires under the brush piles with blocks of dried wood. When the flames became hot enough, the green trees in the brush piles caught on fire as well. As the brush piles burned down, a Cat would push more fuel into the fire.

My experience is that Cat skinning, or operating a Cat, involves working at an unnatural speed, a machine speed, with a piece of equipment that has awesome power to cut down trees and rearrange the environment. The person in the role of the Cat skinner cannot enter into a relationship with the Cat as a teamster did with a team of horses. The teamster and horses have the same aspects of body, mind, emotion, and spirit. They are conditioned to respond to communications emitted through these aspects. A Cat does not get tired of working as its operator does, whereas a work team of horses and its teamster get tired in proportion to the work they perform. Both require rest and nourishment to replace their energy.

The teamster and his horses can enter into a relationship as living beings with the land, plants, and animals. A Cat generates excessive heat and fumes from burning fuel. It is ironic that its energy is measured in horsepower. A Cat skinner working a Cat in a ten-hour shift feels exhausted from being violently shaken, inhaling fumes, and having no personal contact with others during this working period. He becomes disoriented and alienated from others, and requires time to heal and regain the balance of his body, mind, emotion, and spirit with natural beings. My operators would return home in the late evening, between 7:00 p.m. and 8:00 p.m., and usually eat supper alone, as their families would have already eaten. They would be able to socialize with their families for a brief time, and maybe recite an evening prayer with them before retiring for the night. The next day my operators would rise and perform this ritual again, a cycle which continued until the construction work was completed or the construction season was over.

My day was much longer. I had more responsibilities than my work crew and so slept only five to six hours a day. I had to ensure that the equipment was in good working order, do the payroll, invoice the oil company for payment, purchase supplies such as fuel and food, and prepare bids for future work. My work schedule was seven days a week for the entire four-month winter oilfield program, in order to earn enough money to make my company profitable. During this time I discovered that it was much easier to drink alcohol during the day for an immediate high to escape the stress of my responsibilities and work load rather than to take the time out for my prayers and spiritual needs. Alcohol could dull my emotions and spirituality. It also allowed me to become "one of the boys" in this game with the oilmen. When the oilfield construction season was over, at spring breakup in March, I turned to farming my father's land for the summer.

THE SEASON OF MECHANIZED FARMING

U PON retirement, my father had rented out his land allotment to a farmer from the Settlement because none of my older brothers were interested in farming. In return, he got a one-third share of the crop. When I returned to my home community, I discovered the family farm to be in such a condition of neglect that I had difficulty recognizing it.

All the barns had been dismantled to be used as firewood by my parents. The poplar rails and willow fence posts that had once formed the corrals and fences had rotted and fallen over. The farmers who were renting the land had not cleaned their seed grains, and the once-clean grain fields were contaminated with wild oats, Canada thistle, and quack grass. Farming was now completely mechanized, and tractors and modern farm equipment had replaced the horses and horse-drawn equipment. If I wanted to become a farmer, I would have to buy a complete set of used farm equipment, clean the farm, and learn from my father how to grain farm.

Learning the Industrial Tools of Farming

The process of dismantling the old fences and the remaining old farm buildings, repairing the granaries, and visiting farm auction sales and used farm-equipment dealers took an entire month. I had decided to purchase used John Deere farm equipment, because this equipment had a reputation for never wearing out and requiring minimum maintenance and repair. My father taught me how to use the equipment. He showed me how to set the four-bottom hydraulic plow to plow furrows at an even depth of six inches, how to begin the first furrow by pacing off a section of land forty paces wide (120 feet), and where to install markers at each end of the field to be used as guideposts.

I began plowing the field at one end while aiming the tractor for the guidepost at the other end. Meanwhile, my eighty-six-year-old father walked slowly behind the plow, measuring the furrow depth with a metal carpenter's tape measure. Once he had set the plowshares and coulters to his satisfaction, he would sit along the field on a wooden chair and watch me plow his old field. During my lunch breaks and in the evenings, he would instruct me on what activity had to be done after the plowing of the field was completed. I slowly began to reacquire my parent's traditional ecological knowledge.

My father and I jointly decided that I should plant a variety of ninety-day barley as a cash grain crop. This meant that from the time of seeding, the crop would mature to the stage of being harvested in ninety days. This eliminated the risk of its freezing from a late spring or early fall frost. I planted and harvested an eighty-acre field that adjoined my parents' farmhouse, and summer-fallowed a forty-acre field about six miles from there. My father recognized that I could not enter into a relationship with the land as he had. I felt detached from the land, and treated it like something that was inanimate and lifeless. I viewed the land as a commodity, rather than as a gift, which I could use to make a living by harvesting a cash crop. My father informed me that If I could not develop a "feel" for the land, then it was best to rent it to others for a third of the crop, as he had done.

My father asked me if I had ever dreamed about farming, and I told him that I had not. My father's view of farming was that a tractor caused a modern farmer to speed up the farming activities. The process was now too fast to allow enough time for the farmer to enter into a relationship with the land that he was cultivating. This new farming method was about two-thirds faster than the old method of farming with horses. This meant that a farmer worked less in his field. In my father's view, this shortened time frame, combined with treating the land as a commodity, was what kept me emotionally and spiritually detached from it.

COMMENTARY

BY making a living *off* the land through natural gas field construction and grain farming, I had entered into a social relationship with the people with whom I worked, but not with the land and its plants and animals. I had accepted an outside view of the land as an object. The answer to the question about whether natural gas development would have positive impacts for employment and business opportunities turned out to be affirmative for those who became involved in this work. Those people, including me – because the nature of this work was cutting, piling and burning brush – accepted the view that these plants were objects that had to be removed in this manner for progress to occur. At that time, such a process did not warrant the oil company's conducting an environmental impact assess-ment review. Thus, those like my father who were concerned about negative impacts on their sacred relationship with the land were ignored, and their issues were not dealt with.

My father did not officially retire because of an old age retirement policy, but because his body, no longer mobile, could not perform the activities of his mind, emotion, and spirit. He continued, in the Metis way of doing things, to give advice and spiritual guidance to those who sought his trad-itional knowledge about the concept of spiritual exchange until the day he passed into the spirit world.

To succeed at my work, I had learned to make the personal and spiritual compromises necessary to influence oil company executives, contractors, Settlement councillors, and business-men. The concept of spiritual exchange had been repressed and had disappeared from my daily life and my livelihood.

CHAPTER FOUR: THE PATH TO REVITALIZATION

SUMMARY

THESE two different ways of making a living within the community of the Paddle Prairie Metis Settlement were separated by sixteen years. These sixteen years are marked by the "progress" made by the community in order to support its growing population.

Living with the Land

The first livelihood described contained a local traditional worldview of a living universe. This universe, created by The Great Spirit, comprises three worlds: the spirit world, this world, and the evil world. These worlds were blended together one on top of the other. The Great Spirit then created other spirits, including Our Father, Our Mother, Our Grandfathers, and Our Grandmothers, for assistance in providing harmony and balance to the three worlds. These spirits were gifted with the spiritual power to transform or shape-shift into different forms of spirit helpers and messengers. Those spirit messengers who appeared in dreams were also gifted with powers to take the forms of spiritual and evil forces of this world.

Dream spirits brought the gift of life, containing the aspects of the spirit, the mind, and emotion, from the spirit world to the body. These aspects allow the existence of living beings, a category which includes plants and animals. All living beings were seen as having a life cycle of birth and death, possessing spiritual and evil forces, and being interdependent and equal to one another. People were created as one of these living beings. Their challenge, in order to live a happy and healthy life, was to keep their aspects of spirit, mind, emotion, and body in harmony and balance through the use of food. The Great Spirit created food as a gift, something that was freely exchanged and shared between a donor and recipient through the relationships of giving and receiving.

Different forms of gifts or food were required for the different aspects of a human being. Food for the body consisted of gifts of air, water, meat, fruit, etc. Food for the mind consisted of gifts of creating, thinking, learning, etc. Food for the emotions consisted of gifts of love, happiness, anger, pain, etc. Food for the spirit consisted of gifts of the powers of giving, receiving, and sharing. These gifts were acquired through the activities of ceremony, ritual, and sacrifice performed within a proper context.

Ceremony was the physical movement of the body performed by a person in order to make a living. Ritual was the repeated patterns of behaviour using the mind and emotion in order to make a living. Sacrifice was the offering and requesting of life from a plant or animal for use as food. These activities were accomplished through continuous relationships established by gift exchanges. Gifts were both the intangible and the tangible expressions of the exchange of aspects of the mind, emotion, spirit, and body between a donor and a recipient. The concept of spiritual exchange was referred to as "Spirit Gifting" and underlay one's relationship with the land that included gathering and harvesting gifts of plants and animals.

This relationship with the land was put into motion by a seasonal round of living, patterned after a Metis calendar. This calendar was made up of natural signs that signalled the beginning of activities involving the planting, gathering, and harvesting of plants and animals. The essence of this relationship was primarily spiritual, as it was based upon the local traditions of ceremony, ritual, and sacrifice for the preparation and sharing of the gifts of food obtained from the land.

The Great Spirit and spirits from the spirit world were the donors of these gifts, of the aspects of the mind, emotion, spirit, and body of plants and animals. This concept of "Spirit Gifting" was incorporated into every activity of livelihood. This concept was noticeably absent from the second livelihood: making a living *off* the land.

Living off the Land

The second livelihood consisted of a secular view of the universe and the absence of a sense of the sacred. This lively-hood involved obtaining contract work for the construction of a natural gas field and farming alone with heavy machinery.

During my construction work, wild plants and animals were not viewed as gifts created by The Great Spirit. One had to treat them as things to be destroyed and removed, so that deposits of natural gas could be extracted by a multinational oil company for sale. In this mode of production it was assumed that only human beings possess consciousness and the ability to think rationally. A second premise was that a person could never fulfill his or her material needs without entering into social relationships with certain people in positions of power. These social relationships were conscious and played a for-mative role in structuring the process of producing natural gas. In this livelihood an individual Metis, as a contractor, could play only a limited role.

The landman, an employee of the multinational oil company, initiated the process by requesting permission from the Settlement Council for right-of-entry onto Settlement land for the purpose of developing a natural gas field. This request was based upon the oil company's worldview that it had pur-chased mineral rights to subsurface resources from the provincial government. The membership of the Metis Settlement, on the other hand, viewed itself as receiving the land as a gift from the Great Spirit, the creator of the land. This conflict of worldviews still has to be resolved.

The Settlement decided to give permission for right-of-entry to the oil company provided that individual Metis contractors were allowed to bid on construction work, including the clear-cutting, piling, and burning of the brush. Individual Metis who were awarded this work purchased construction equipment and hired people to do the work. Social relationships developed by the Metis contractors with oilmen sometimes jeopardized lifelong friendships with their fellow Metis. As a result of lobbying and competing for construction contracts, the Metis contractor did not have time to gather and harvest wild plants and animals for food and did not have the time to enter into a relationship with the land.

In the process of operating the Cat at a machine speed, a difference in sense of time developed that did not allow the Metis Cat skinner to develop a sacred and constant relationship with the land. This, in turn, created an atmosphere of working *off* the land rather than *with* the land. This secular atmosphere allowed the Cat skinner to view the land as an object, a commodity for exchange, to be dominated by man and machine. My experience is that this view of the land carried over when I turned to farming after the construction season in the oilfield came to an end.

CONCLUSION

THIS narrative has emphasized that changes in subsistence patterns caused some of the Metis of Paddle Prairie, in-cluding me, to repress their sacred worldview and the way they related *with* the land through spiritual exchange. In my own case, this resulted in a dissatisfaction so intense that it stim-ulated me to attempt to revitalize my repressed worldview. In this concluding chapter, I will attempt to frame what happened to me from an anthropological perspective.

I was somewhat unsuccessful in searching the anthropological literature for a suitable model to analyze my own self-revitalization process. For example, I concluded that Marcel Mauss's *The Gift*, on the concept of reciprocity – to give, to receive, and to repay – did not adequately address this central question: "What power resides in the object given that causes its recipient to pay it back?" (Mauss, 1990:3). I also discovered that anthropologists have focused primarily upon group revitalization rather than individual revitalization. As my motivation for writing this narrative was to try to understand the revitalization of the concept of spiritual exchange in my own daily life as an individual, I have had to construct my own model. Before presenting my model of the individual, I will briefly describe the group model proposed by Anthony Wallace (1970).

A Model of Group Revitalization

According to Anthony Wallace (1970:188), the revitalization movement of a group can be defined as "deliberate, organized attempts by some members of a society to construct a more satisfying culture by rapid acceptance of a pattern of multiple innovations." In general, revitalization processes share a common structure that can be conceptualized as a pattern of temporally overlapping but functionally distinct stages. During the first stage, what Wallace calls the "Steady State," change occurs at a relatively slow pace, and levels of social disorganization and stress remain within tolerable limits.

In the second stage, the "Period of Increased Individual Stress," the socio-cultural system is "pushed" progressively out of equilibrium by forces such as disease, conquest, or internal decay. Increasingly, large numbers of individuals are placed under intolerable stress, and disillusionment becomes widespread. This disillusionment is reflected in social indices such as increased crime and suicide rates.

In the third stage, the "Period of Cultural Distortion," some societal members attempt, ineffectively, to restore personal equilibrium by adopting socially dysfunctional coping strategies such as alcoholism and gambling. In the second stage, such strategies are regarded as individual deviancies; in the third stage, as interest groups attempt to circumvent the evil effects of "the system," these strategies become institutionalized.

Conditions can worsen to the point that the population will die off, splinter into autonomous groups, or be absorbed into another, more stable society unless the culture as a whole is revitalized.

Revitalization (the fourth stage) will depend upon the successful completion of the following six steps:

- **Formulation of a Code:** An individual or a group of individuals construct(s) a new utopian image of a "goal culture," which is contrasted with the existing culture. Connecting the existing culture and goal culture is a "transfer culture." This serves as a system of operations that will transform the existing culture into the goal culture.

- **Communication:** The formulators of the code attempt to win converts. Converts are promised the benefits of a more highly organized system, whereas refusal to accept the code is depicted as a sure formula for disaster.

- **Organization:** As new converts are attracted, they fall into two groups: a set of disciples who administer the program, and the followers. If the original code was formulated by a single individual, he or she is increaseingly regarded as a prophet who requires unwavering allegiance.

- **Adaptation:** As problems with the original code and how it is applied become apparent, the code is reworked and defended. Eventually, however, the code becomes institutionalized, and anyone who challenges the code is regarded as a traitor.

- **Cultural Transformation:** If the movement is able to capture the allegiance of a substantial proportion of the population, it may be possible to put the goal culture into operation, leading to the revitalization of the group.

- **Routinization:** If revitalization is successful, the revolutionary function of the prophet's movement shifts from innovation to maintenance.

In the final stage, the "New Steady State," the group returns to a "normal" condition characterized by steady-state processes of change.

A Model of Individual Revitalization

My own model of individual revitalization is diagrammed in Figure 1. I hope that this model will be useful for the self-appraisal of individuals who may be going through the same process I went through. I will discuss each stage represented in the model.

- **Traditional Knowledge:** Traditional knowledge, as I know it, refers to the body of information, rules, and values which made existence possible and meaningful for a Metis group of people before they were overwhelmed by the influence of foreign codes. Traditional knowledge may incorporate outside influences, but it retains an integrity of its own. The traditional knowledge of Paddle Prairie Metis is described in Chapter 2. This form of knowledge constituted my first worldview.

The essential elements of my Metis traditional knowledge are depicted in Table 1. This knowledge involved a sacred worldview in which The Great Spirit, who can also be conceived as Our Creator, Our Father, or Our Mother, created spirit helpers and messengers, referred to as Our Grandfathers and Our Grandmothers. Our Creator also created land as a gift, referred to as Mother Earth. Plants, people, and other animals were also viewed as gifts because they were part of the land. Relationships between the people and the other gifts were characterized by spiritual exchanges which continually renew the body, mind, emotion, and spirit.

Our way of making a living was *with* the land. The land was used only for basic subsistence with a small surplus, rather than for profit, and use of the land was marked by an ongoing round of ceremonies, rituals, and sacrifices. The gifts from Mother Earth were viewed in concrete terms, and ownership was viewed as collective stewardship. The essence of this holistic livelihood was sharing, giving, and receiving in an attempt to keep body, mind, emotion, and spirit in balance. To the extent that this was done, the individual existed in a spiritual state, and was happy and healthy.

As changes occurred in what I was learning and in my subsistence patterns, I began to repress my codes of traditional knowledge and to adopt the codes of Western knowledge.

- **Adoption of Western Scientific Knowledge:** What I received from Western scientific knowledge included a secular worldview of nature (land and living beings) as evolving from a "big bang" and a "black hole." I began to view nature as an object and man as separated from the land. My relation to the land was characterized by adaptation, domination and individual ownership. My way of making a living was *off* the land rather than *with* the land. Planning for the future, rather than living for the present, I used technology to change the gifts of the land into products and commodities of exchange for an abstract value known as currency. The ultimate goal was materialism and the acquisition of wealth. My livelihood was achieved by juggling different roles: cultural, political, economic, and social.

Adopting technology such as "Cats" was relatively easy, because these machines made it easier and faster to destroy and rearrange ecosystems during the construction of a natural gas field. During this period of my life, I did not have the time to evaluate my beliefs and practices involving the rape and exploitation of the gifts of Mother Earth.

- **Introspection and Self-Appraisal:** As a result of my dissatisfaction, I undertook a comparative analysis and interpretation of the two sources of my personal knowledge, traditional and Western (shown in Table 1). This personal knowledge formed the essential codes relating to my behaviour and human values. "Human values [are] the basis upon which an individual chooses one course over another [and] judges some things as better or worse, right or wrong" (Lee, 1976:5). This comparison involved a self-appraisal of two events of my life history using the concept of the ideal self.

- **Formulation of a Concept of the Ideal Self:** The construct of the ideal self consists of interrelated statements about the bases, structure, and functional implications of self-appraisal (Watson and Watson-Franke, 1985:187). It assumes that in any society, a set of normative (emic) statements about ideal or proper behaviour (personality functioning) is built into a wide range of diverse statuses. Measuring up to the codes of the ideal self becomes a vital component in the way role behaviour is articulated or phrased in meeting the demands of interpersonal situations (Watson and Watson-Franke, 1985:188).

The cognitive dimension of the ideal self involves the psychological process of self-appraisal by which an individual, in a way meaningful to himself or herself, draws upon the codes of the ideal self to evaluate his or her own behaviours so that he or she can change it in a more personally relevant, socially acceptable direction (Watson and Watson-Franke, 1985:189).

The behavioural dimension of the ideal self involves modifying and correcting the many roles we constantly juggle as we attempt to work them out in a cultural context until they assume an equivalent emic significance (Watson and Watson-Franke, 1985:190). For example, we must sometimes "take a long second look at, and seriously examine, the role that material wealth plays in taking us away from our responsibilities to Our Creator" (Cardinal, 1977:222).

- **Rediscovery of the Concept of Spiritual Exchange:** During the process of self-appraisal, using the concept of the ideal self (what I really wanted to be), I rediscovered a repressed code from my traditional knowledge, the concept of spiritual exchange, which I now refer to as "Spirit Gifting." I revitalized this concept as a part of my way of knowing to form a new code which blends both traditional and Western scientific knowledge in a way that had been impossible for me before.

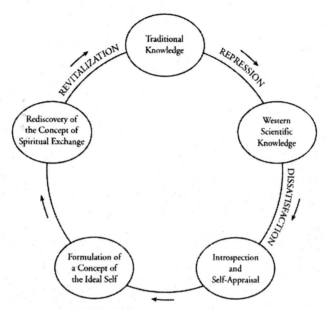

Figure 1: A Model of the Process of Individual Revitalization

Figure 1 Revitalization Model

Traditional Knowledge

- Emic modes of thought predominate.

- Experiential interpretation of behaviour gives the subjective meaning of reality.

- In this sacred worldview, The Great Spirit, Our Creator, created land as living beings that are viewed as gifts.

- People are viewed as a part of the land; their relationships with the land create a renewal of spirituality through exchanges.

- People live *with* the land for today and this moment.

- Spirituality, sharing, giving, and receiving are the essence.

- The subsistence pattern is supported through ceremony, ritual, and sacrifice.

- A gift is a concrete value of spiritual exchange.

- Holistic is making a living *with* the land.

- Ownership is collective stewardship.

Figure 2 Traditional Knowledge

Western Scientific Knowledge

- Etic modes of thought predominate.

- Objective interpretation of behaviour gives the scientific meaning of reality.

- In this secular worldview, land and man evolved from a big bang and are viewed as objects.

- People are viewed as separated from the land; their relationships with the land are formed through adaptation..

- People live *off* the land for tomorrow and the next moment.

- Materialism, consumption, and technology are the essence.

- The subsistence pattern is supported through economic growth, profit, and acquisition of wealth.

- A currency is an abstract value of monetary exchange.

- Integrated is making a living *off* the land.

- Ownership is domination.

Figure 3 Western Scientific Knowledge

Comparison of Group and Individual Revitalization Models

It may be useful to compare and contrast the group and individual revitalization models presented here. First, both models emphasize that revitalization is the result of stress and dissatisfaction with an existing culture, which lead to deliberate attempts to construct a more satisfying culture. The main difference is that in the group model, change is initiated by an individual or a group of individuals for the purpose of changing society, whereas in the individual model, change is initiated by one person for his or her own purposes.

Second, both models involve a code and a "goal culture." The group model, however, emphasizes the construction of a new, utopian image of cultural and social organization, whereas the individual model, at least as it applies to my own case, emphasizes the combination of traditional and Western knowledge in light of one's concept of the ideal self.

Third, both models emphasize that codes associated with revitalization provide the means of protecting individuals and groups from anomie during the shift from one cultural phase to another. The main difference is that in the group model, codes protect a society from disintegration and possible extinction, whereas in the individual model, codes protect a person from loss of self-respect and identity.

Finally, in both models, revitalized codes become routinized and, in the process, rebalance the organizational structure of the society and the lives of individuals. The main difference is that in the group model, revitalization transforms a dysfunctional society into a functional one in which a new steady state prevails, whereas in the individual model, revitalization frees repressed aspects of traditional knowledge and allows a new blend of body, mind, emotion, and spirit.

Group and individual models allow us to understand an important aspect of culture change, but at different levels of analysis. The group model has been the most popular in anthropology because of a tendency to concentrate on social processes at the expense of understanding individual psychological processes. The goal here has been to demonstrate that the group model of revitalization can be adapted to help illuminate revitalization at the individual level.

My Present Situation

The changes in subsistence patterns of some of the people in Paddle Prairie, as described in Chapters 2 and 3, involved my willing participation. I did not attempt to resist the shift from a sacred to a secular worldview. This shift in my individual thought worlds does not necessarily reflect the experiences of the entire community, because not all members took part in this shift, nor did all have the same experiences that I had. But I, for one, certainly changed.

This work has involved contemplating, studying, and rethinking these changes at the middle point of my life. This study has helped me in my quest to develop a renewed relationship with the timeless values and principles that have been kept alive for Western society by the very people Western society has tried to destroy (Mander, 1992:384). I no longer view plants and animals as objects, but once again as sacred gifts: living beings, with the same four aspects that I have. For example, if my family requires the harvesting of a medicinal plant to assist us in healing the common cold or flu, we enact the gathering ceremony and its rituals. We thus once again perform the sacrifice of spiritual exchange as my father, aunt, and other ancestors did before us. We also burn sweetgrass and diamond willow fungus, pray, and practice gift exchange at special family occasions and holidays. Every morning and night, I take time to meditate about my daily activities and how to balance them with my four aspects of body, mind, emotion, and spirit. I find the process of revitalizing the concept of spiritual exchanging is never static but always flowing and changing with each new experience and day. I hope my experience will assist those in a similar process of self-appraisal.

I am presently living with my family on an acreage in a semi-rural community, named Winterburn, located on the outskirts of the city of Edmonton, Alberta. My wife Kim and I are self-employed, and work from our home under the company name of Ghostkeeper Synergetics Ltd. We undertake consulting and advising opportunities in a variety of fields. Our three children attend a community school located three miles from the farm. I raise registered Morgan horses for pleasure and sale, and endurance-ride for exercise and sport with a neighbour who lives just down the road. Our family holds an annual horseshoe tournament, barbecue, and barn dance which has become a community event.

Over the past few years, I have come to know many people in our community and discovered that some are going through a process of self-appraisal and individual revitalization similar to my own. Our similar experience has led us to share the concept of belonging both to the community and to the land. Our self-reflection seems to be induced by factors such as the rapidly changing ways of making a living, the shifting from industrialization to information and service-based economies, industry and government cutbacks to control deficits, low interest rates to control inflation, and job layoffs during company restructuring to achieve sustainable development. Such changes mean that one is no longer guaranteed a safe, secure job (although I do wonder if one ever was). The uncertainty concerning how to create and renew economic strategies is stressful and frightening to those people who have lost their livelihoods, as well as to those who still are fortunate enough to have jobs which they find fulfilling, challenging, and rewarding.

I and some of my neighbours are in the process of re-thinking and revitalizing old concepts and creating new ones to provide our families with a sense of security and work during this time of change. In my own case, the revitalization of Spirit Gifting as a concept of spiritual exchange has pro-vided me with a means to care for my family and prepare for the future, without sacrificing the quality of my relationship *with* the land and the other gifts of living beings.

REFERENCES

Asch, M.I. 1979. The ecological-evolutionary model and the concept of mode of production: Two approaches to material reproduction. In: Turner, D.H., and Smith, G.A., eds. *Challenging anthropology: A critical introduction to social and cultural anthropology.* Toronto: McGraw-Hill Ryerson. 81-97.

Cardinal, H. 1977. *The rebirth of Canada's Indians.* Edmonton: Hurtig Publishers.

Dickason, O. 1992. *Canada's First Nations: A History of founding peoples from earliest times.* Toronto: McClelland & Stewart Inc.

Enchanted Learning. As seen March 17, 2006, on http://www.enchantedlearning.com/subjects/dinosaurs/mesozoic/Cretaceous.html

Lee, D. 1976. *Valuing the self: What we can learn from other cultures.* Prospect Heights, Illinois: Waveland Press Inc.

Mander, J. 1992. *In absence of the sacred: The failure of technology and the survival of Indian Nations.* San Francisco: Sierra Club Books.

Mauss, M. 1990. *The gift: Forms and functions of exchange in archaic societies.* Translated by W.D. Halls. Forward by Mary Douglas. New York: W.W. Norton.

McCully, A., and Seaton, H. 1982. *Paddle Prairie Metis Settlement land use planning inventory.* Edmonton: Alberta Municipal Affairs Planning Branch.

Swannell, J., Ed 1992. *Oxford Modern English Dictionary.* Oxford, New York, Toronto: Oxford University Press.

The Metis in Alberta website. Ewing Commission. As seen March 16, 2006, at http://www.albertasource.ca/metis/ eng/people_and_communities/issues_ewing_commission.h tm

Wallace, A. 1970. *Culture and personality.* 2nd ed. New York: Random House, Inc.

Watson, L., and Watson-Franke, M. 1985. *Interpreting life histories: An anthropological inquiry.* New Brunswick, New Jersey: Rutgers University Press.

ENGLISH INDEX

T

W

CREE GLOSSARY

ABOUT THE AUTHOR

ELMER Ghostkeeper grew up on a farm on the Paddle Prairie Metis Settlement. His family worked *with* the land using horses rather than mechanized farm vehicles. Their syncretic spirituality supported their lives and livelihoods. After grade nine, Elmer left the Settlement to complete his high school in Fairview, Alberta. From there, he upgraded some grade twelve courses at Alberta College in Edmonton and then went to the Northern Alberta Institute of Technology where he achieved a diploma in Civil Engineering Technology. His work in the engineering field took him to Whitehorse where he held the jobs of assistant city engineer, survey technologist, and concrete, soil and asphalt technologist. He returned to Paddle Prairie in 1974, and for a short period, worked the family farm.

In 1980, Elmer achieved a Bachelor of Arts in Anthropology at the University of Alberta. He was selected for the Canadian Young Achiever Award to attend the Canadian Constitution repatriation ceremonies in Ottawa in 1982. In 1995, he achieved a Master of Arts degree in Anthropology; *Spirit Gifting* was his thesis. While working on his MA, Elmer received the Ralph Steinhauer Award of Distinction in recognition of exceptional academic achievement.

From 1980 to 1984, Elmer was the President of the Alberta Federation of Metis Settlement Associations. He has also held the position of Chair of the Aboriginal Learning Sub-Committee, been a member of a Learning Alberta Steering Committee, Advanced Education, and was the Research Policy Officer, Metis Centre, National Aboriginal Health Organization. In 2004, Elmer received the Order of the Metis Nation.

Today, Elmer is the President and Chief Operating Officer of Metis Moccasin Resources Inc., an oil and natural gas exploration and production company. He is also in the process of building Spirit Wisdom Lodge, a retreat for holistic reflection and healing located on the shores of Buffalo Lake, Buffalo Metis Settlement, in North Eastern Alberta.

PUBLISH WITH US

IF you are interested in submitting your manuscript to Writing on Stone Press, please see our website at www.writingonstone.ca for submission guidelines.

We are actively accepting manuscripts for all types of non-fiction books, and some fiction books. See our website for specific requests for submissions.

NOTE FROM THE PUBLISHER

Our Press is dedicated to quality publishing. If you find any errors in this book, please feel free to contact us at info@writingonstone.ca, and we will do our best to correct the error.

CPSIA information can be obtained at www.ICGtesting.com
Printed in the USA
LVOW07s0530121016

508447LV00001B/7/P